The COINAGE *of* ROMAN BRITAIN

The Coinage of Roman Britain

Richard Reece

TEMPUS

First published 2002
Reprinted 2006

Tempus Publishing Limited
The Mill, Brimscombe Port,
Stroud, Gloucestershire, GL5 2QG
www.tempus-publishing.com

British Library Cataloguing in Publication Data.
A catalogue record for this book is available from the British Library.

ISBN 0 7524 2523 4

Typesetting and origination by Tempus Publishing Limited.
Printed in Great Britain.

Contents

List of illustrations 7

Preface: No numbers 9

Introduction 11

1 Coinage in the Roman world (in 21 easy stages) 13

2 Coinage in Roman Britain 37

3 Hoards 67

4 Site-finds 89

5 The use of Roman coins 107

6 Britain and abroad 129

Appendix 1 Archaeology 141

Appendix 2 Numbers 145

Further reading 151

Index 155

List of illustrations

A ★ denotes a coin in the Ashmolean Museum; all others are private collections.
All photographs by the author, © Richard Reece, except **colour plate 23**, © a colleague

1 Moneyer's as of Augustus★
2 Denarius of Nero (pre-AD 64)★
3 Denarius of Nero (post-AD 64)★
4 Denarius of Domitian
5 Sestertius of Hadrian★
6 Sestertius of Postumus★
7 Radiate of Postumus
8 Radiate of Aurelian★
9 Urbs Roma
10 Gloria Exercitus 330-5★
11 Solidus of Constantius II★
12 Gratian, Gloria Novi Saeculi
13 Late silver★
14 Late gold★
15 Late copper
16 Late copper
17 Sestertius of Antoninus Pius★
18 As of Antoninus Pius
19-28 Coins struck by Carausius★
29 Allectus
30 Silver coin of Constantius II★
31 Silver coin of Julian★
32 Solidus of Magnus Maximus★
33 Sestertius of Antoninus Pius
34 Sestertius of Commodus
35 Denarius of Julia Paula
36 Sestertius of Otacilia Severa★
37 Radiate of Trajan Decius
38 Radiate of Gallienus
39 Tetradrachm of Diocletian
40 Fel Temp Reparatio, phoenix★
41 The Roman currency system in use in the first century AD★
42 Denarius of Tiberius★
43 The decline of the currency system between about AD 1 and AD 260 as shown by the sestertius★
44 Silvered bronze of Constantine I
45 Copper of Theodora
46 Copper of Divo Constantino

Colour plates

1 The main coins of the period AD 1 to 400 shown at twice their actual size
2 Aureus of Claudius*
3 Copies of the As of Claudius I showing Minerva (c)*
4 Denarius of Marc Antony*
5 Denarius of Marc Antony
6 Denarius of Marc Antony
7 Silver drachma of Trajan
8 Sestertius of Commodus
9 Plated denarius of the Roman republic (56 BC)
10 Plated denarius of Severus Alexander (222-35)
11 Die-linked denarii of Augustus*
12 Aurei of Faustina I*
13 Aureii of Marcus Aurelius, about AD 155 and 175*
14 Denarius of Hadrian
15 Radiate and denarius of Caracalla*
16 Gold coin of Postumus*
17 Gold coin of Gallienus*
18 Gold coins of Gallienus
19 Radiates of Postumus, Victorinus, Tetricus I and Tetricus II
20 Radiates of Claudius II, and barbarous radiates
21 Base silver radiate of Gallienus, and radiate of Claudius II
22 Gold coin of Carinus and Numerian from Richborough (electrotype)
23 Gold hoard
24 Copper hoard
25 Gold coin of Maximian*
26 Silver coin of Diocletian*
27 Nummus/Follis of Diocletian*
28 Radiate and Laureate of Diocletian*
29 Silver/copper of Constantine I
30 Silver/copper of Constantius II
31 Copies of the House of Constantine
32 Constantinople, and a copy
33 Gloria Exercitus, and a copy
34 House of Constantine hybrid reverse
35 House of Constantine hybrid obverse
36 Fel Temp Reparatio fallen horseman*
37 Fallen horseman copy*
38 Two Victories
39 VOT XX/MVLT XXX
40 House of Valentinian, Securitas Reipublicae
41 Coins of Magus Maximus; city gateway and Reparatio Reip
42 Late silver from Trier
43 Solidus of Arcadius from Richborough (electrotype)
44 Solidus of Constantine III*

Preface: no numbers

About forty years ago Barry Cunliffe asked me to prepare for publication the last batch of coins found many years before at the fort of Richborough on the coast of Kent. He also suggested that it would be a good idea if I gathered together information on the 55,000 coins that had been found and said something about them. It was a terrible idea, but I did it, and I have nearly recovered.

The point is that there was no method at the time for extracting information from coins found on a site, there was little information on coins from other sites with which to compare Richborough, and coins outside Britain were almost unknown. I learned as I went along, and made some major mistakes which provided endless amusement when I found out what they were and how to correct them. I hope the summary of how things stand today, in the eyes of just one rather biased observer, will show that things have changed.

The comparison of sites both within Britain and of Britain and abroad has to be both qualitative – are the coins in different places the same coins? – and quantitative – do the same numbers of given coins get to different places? Describing the coins can be done in words, and everyone who is interested is fairly happy to consider the results. Discussing numbers of coins on the other hand has necessarily to be done in numbers, and it has become clear that this excludes a large number of people who are interested in the past; accordingly, this aspect of the work has been followed by only a few.

In this book therefore I have tried to write only in words and to banish all numbers and numerical methods to a few pages of Appendix. I have found this process frustrating, because on many aspects of the subject you can say so much more in a far clearer fashion in numbers and diagrams than you can in words. I can only hope that the result will communicate basic information, ideas and excitement to anyone who is interested. Numero-addicts should be able to find their fix through the books and articles suggested in the section in Further reading.

The illustrations are my own photographs or direct scans, with the exception of **colour plate 23** which was taken by a colleague. Those coins belonging to the Ashmolean Museum are indicated; the others are from excavations and the collections of friends. The cover photograph is courtesy of and copyright Guy de la Bédoyère. To all of these sources I am very grateful.

Many people have helped in the 40-year process of learning, but they are far too many to list here. For help with ideas, comments and questions on the book I must thank Peter Guest, Matt Ponting, Tim Clarke, Kevin Butcher, Nick Somerton and Neil Holbrook.

Introduction

The subject matter of this book is quite easy to define: coins of the Roman period found in Britain. One approach, the most unimaginative and the most informative – surprising how these two often go together – would be a list that would tell you what Roman coins have been found in Britain. This is no good: why? Because you want to try to understand them and then use that understanding to add to your picture either of Roman coins, or of Roman Britain, or both.

There was a slight difference in the way I phrased things just now – Roman coins and coins of the Roman period. This is to allow for all the millions of coins brought to Britain from mints throughout the empire, and the millions of copies of those coins that the Britons made for themselves. These points settle the contents of the first two chapters. First we have to find out what the Roman state was producing in the way of coinage, how it changed, how it developed, how it stumbled; and then we have to set out what Roman coinage came to Britain and what the Britons did for themselves. These subjects have been studied for centuries, and ideas have been batted round, revised, improved and edited so that what we have now are probably fairly close to facts. Where I see room for improvement, or change, or just disruption, I will try to say so; otherwise details are fairly safe.

In a sense these two chapters can stand in place of the list. Before we can investigate ideas, we need to know what form our evidence for coinage in Roman Britain takes. Most coins now in museums or collections which were found in Britain belong either to hoards – coins deposited in a group – or to groups found singly during excavation or walking over fields. The two classes are very different and need to be examined separately, especially when we start to interpret them. Hence chapter 3 on hoards and chapter 4 on site-finds.

We can then consider in chapter 5 how those coins were used and what the rules are for interpretation. There are all sorts of different ways of looking into this, so quotations from the Gospels rub shoulders with the contents of rubbish pits. The basis for comment has changed radically from chapter 1, which I suggested was fairly near to statement of fact; ideas on the use of coins contain few statements and even fewer facts. They depend on interpretation, which is basically the testing of inspiration against the evidence. Even worse, the way forward is to ask questions rather than to accept statements.

In chapter 6 I suggest we look abroad. Some people get worried about this because it represents the great unknown; yet so long as we have the basis of chapter 1, we are well equipped to look at foreign cities and museums and to note the differences between Britain and The Rest – even for Roman times.

Two appendices include very short summaries of technical detail: how do coins actually occur on excavations and what can we know about them? What happens when you stop using words and start using numbers to discuss coin finds? Neither summary gets anywhere; it is simply a statement that the problems are there. Either one could be expanded to form a complete book, and while the coins found on different sites could be made readable the audience for numbers is very limited. Finally, the Further reading section provides some practical suggestions.

1 Coinage in the Roman world (in 21 easy stages)

The West from Augustus to 294

(1) Up to AD 41

The Roman Empire developed out of the Roman Republic, which in turn grew out of a city made up of several villages perched on hills near the river Tiber in Italy. Rome was a late starter in coinage by about 200 years – perhaps because it was a Greek invention and therefore under suspicion. Once the Republic took to coinage it lived on solid copper coins called asses, smaller copper coins which were parts of an as, and good silver coins which got their name when there were ten asses to the denarius: decem, ten, and thus denarius, tenner.

In the first of a long chain of monetary changes the amount of money in circulation was raised by 60% by the simple act of making every denarius worth 16 asses. This seems to have happened in a very short time, somewhere around 140 BC, and the only people who could have suffered were those who had all their savings stored in a pot in copper asses: when they went out to the money-changer to buy a silver coin to pay some tax they would have to take 16 asses instead of 10. In fact, so far as we know, people who did store their wealth as coin very sensibly used silver for the purpose. This had an intrinsic value – it was worth very close to its weight in silver – and any account-book changes could not alter that.

Republican copper need not worry us any further here. Since Britain only became officially a part of the Empire in AD 43, and Republican copper seems never to have been transported to Britain, we can note its existence and leave it on one side. It circulated within the Roman world BC at a token rate, and this seems to have ensured that little went beyond the limits of the state. The copper in 16 asses could not buy the same amount of goods as the silver in one denarius. Even if such coins had been seen in independent Britain, the British are unlikely to have had any interest in foreign lumps of copper which circulated at a highly inflated value.

Republican silver was usually struck in Rome by a team of junior magistrates, three appointed each year, who seem to have had control over what the coins showed (the types) and what the writing on them (the legends) said. In the first century BC the system began to change, as military men took over

1 *A moneyer's as of Augustus. All the design is taken up with SC, Senatus Consulto, by decree of the Senate, the name C Asinius Gallus, and his title III VIR AAA FF – part of the three man committee (IIIVIR) overseeing the casting and striking (FF) of gold, silver and bronze (AAA)*

the power that had always existed for the Imperator (the leader of the armed forces) to strike coin in order to pay his troops. Caesar, Pompey and Marc Antony all used this power, and it ran almost unchecked throughout the Civil Wars. Out of these emerged Julius Caesar's great-nephew and adopted son Octavian. He became Augustus and, in spite of his protestations that he was restoring the Republic, the Empire was born.

Virtually all the republican silver was of good standard (at least 95% silver), with the exception of that struck by Marc Antony (mid 80s%), at a time when he was anxious to pay his troops just before his great bid for power in the battle of Actium in 31 BC. The writer Pliny gave a warning about this, claiming Antony 'mixed iron with his silver', and this coinage was discriminated against ever afterwards – but Pliny was wrong. In fact such mixing is impossible by the methods available to the Romans: even if they had been able to melt iron, and had run in some molten silver it would have boiled away immediately (**colour plates 4-6**).

Augustus kept up the earlier standard of silver and the idea of the copper as (**1**). From the Republican coinage he retained only two of the fractions of the as, the half (semis) and the quarter (quadrans). He added the double as or dupondius, and the four as piece, or quarter of a denarius, the large sestertius. The dupondius and the sestertius were both struck in a mixture of copper and zinc, which we know as brass, and which when fresh from the mint would have a glow like gold (if a bit brassy). This is rarely seen today because modern collectors want their coins to look old and respectable, not new and brassy, so cleaning and polishing such coins removes much of their market value. The last change Augustus made was to settle the gold piece, the aureus, as a regularly struck part of the coinage worth 25 denarii. This completes the basic system of the early empire (**41**, **colour plate 1**).

Different emperors struck very different amounts of coinage, and throughout the reign of one emperor there were major fluctuations in what was produced and in what amounts. Augustus struck many tons of copper to form a very large number of asses, but his semisses and sestertii are less common. Tiberius struck good amounts of silver and copper.

(2) 41-54

Claudius struck bronze early in his reign; and then for some reason the issues ceased. His silver and gold are not common. He closed down most of the remaining mints in the western provinces, notably in Spain, and concentrated production in Rome (**colour plate 2**).

(3) 54-69

Nero followed on from Claudius and struck very little bronze in the early part of his reign; then suddenly, in about 64, he produced enormous quantities of all the bronze and copper values. Lyon in the centre of France was an important second mint. At the same time he changed the standard of gold and silver (**2 & 3**), and there are far more examples of these available today than of his earlier issues.

2 *(left) Silver denarius of Nero (54-68) before the coinage reform of around AD 64*

3 *(right) Silver denarius of Nero after the coinage reform of 64. The designs of* **2** *and* **3** *are quite different, so that there was no doubt about which coin had the heavier weight and the higher silver content. The young portrait makes it fairly clear, but the head of the earlier coin is bare, while the later has a laurel wreath. In the earlier coin the letters read from right to left, the later coin from left to right*

4 *Denarius of Domitian (81-96) with a good set of dates. Around the figure of Minerva there is the information IMP XIIII COS XIIII CENS P PP – hailed as IMPerator for the 14th time, COnSul for the 14th time, Perpetual CENSor, Pater Patriae (father of the country). This gives a firm date of AD 88*

When there is a change of standard, either in weight or in bullion content, it is almost impossible at present to say anything in detail about numbers of coins produced for the issues 'before' and 'after'. This is because the moment a smaller or baser version of a given coin (the denarius for example) is produced, the larger or better version is worth more than it needs to be; it has more bullion to form the same purchasing power. The state stands to gain if it can get hold of 18 old coins and recycle them as 20 new coins – but so does the private metal-worker. This means that immediately after a known change the better coinage is quickly winkled out of circulation. The 'before' and 'after' issues may have been struck in similar quantities, but the latter will be far more common today.

AD 69, the 'year of the four emperors' when four contenders battled it out for the empire after the death of Nero, produced no major changes in the coinage.

(4) 69-96

Vespasian won the battle and his family ruled the empire until 96. The coinage had a chance to settle down and there were no long-term shifts. Just once, so far as we know, an emperor improved the coinage without changing the purchasing power: Domitian around the year 83. People got to know of this and these coins are far less common today, because they were extracted from circulation quickly. Otherwise Vespasian and his sons produced standard coinage in standard amounts at Rome, and also at Lyon for part of the time (**4**). This coinage is usually very well dated by the emperor's year in office

(6th regnal year: TR P VI), and even these yearly dates are often subdivided by a notice that he held the consulship (3rd time: COS III), or was hailed as Imperator after a particular victory (for the 10th time: IMP X). This means that the fluctuation of coinage can be followed year by year, or even more closely.

(5) 96-117

Two years under Nerva give little to mention, and then comes the reign of Trajan. We have one written reference to him in relation to coins which makes him sound a public spirited emperor: Trajan called in the old worn coins and issued new ones instead. However, judging by the coins that disappear from hoards just a bit later than this time, those he recalled were the Republican denarii, which had about 95% silver. The new issues had rather less, perhaps in the mid 80s %, so this was a good financial move. A very small issue of the old Republican coin types with a legend round to say that they really belonged to the reign of Trajan may have 'made up for' the old coins that had been lost – but this issue was so small that it would only have been enough for one presentation set to each of the old families in Rome on New Year's Day. That is sheer supposition, but it fits.

Trajan's coinage in general was very well produced whether in gold, silver, bronze or copper. The flans (round blanks on which the coins were struck) were well prepared, the lettering was possibly at peak standard, and portraiture was excellent. The lettering needed to be good because Trajan seems to have been eager to get more details about himself on his coins than most did. Apart from all the usual types (designs), Trajan showed a lot of buildings, mostly in Rome – he was clearly proud of his building programme, some of which, like the Markets of Trajan, is still visible today.

(6) 117-38

Hadrian left the standard of the coinage very much as he inherited it from his adoptive father Trajan. His particular interest was in the provinces of the empire, and there are several series of coin issues which show many provincial symbols for the first time; so Britannia appeared, sitting on stones with a shield with a curved knife in the centre, while Mauretania (NW Africa) had a horse with her (the province was famed for the breeding of this animal). There is a whole gallery of types commemorating the emperor's ceremonial arrival in the province (Adventus Aug in X) (**5**), commemorating the army in the province (Exercitus X), or the way the emperor had restored the province after troubles or disasters (Restitutor X).

(7) 138-61

Hadrian, himself adopted by Trajan, in turn adopted Antoninus, who became emperor (Augustus), and then had a struggle with the senate over whether on his death Hadrian should be regarded as a god or not. He won the struggle

5 *Hadrian (117-38) not only spent a lot of time travelling round the provinces, but commemorated the fact on coins. On this sestertius the Emperor on the left is being greeted by Britannia on the right. The legend ADVENTVS AVG BRITANNIAE simply states 'the ceremonial arrival of the emperor in Britain'.*

and for his 'right thinking' he was given the title Pius. So although he was known as Antoninus the Pius One (the meaning is not really the same as our word pious), his coins always take into account the sequence in which things happened: Antoninus Augustus Pius (for coins saying Antoninus Pius see phase 10).

By this stage the silver coins were being less well prepared and struck, the standard of silver may well have been falling slightly, and the fractions of the as, the semis (half) and quadrans (quarter) had for practical purposes almost vanished. It is tempting to suggest that over the 100 years from AD 50-150 prices had risen and so pushed the smallest coins out of use, either because you no longer needed them at the market stall, or they cost more to produce than they were worth. If the latter was the case then, wanted or not, the state was most unlikely to pay for them to be struck. The main Roman idea of minting money was to make money.

(8) 161-80

The coinage of Marcus Aurelius runs smoothly on from that of Antoninus Pius because succession was once again through adoption, and the young prince took office under his adoptive father. He provides one of the best examples of an emperor who is shown ageing year by year, from a curly headed, clean shaven youth to a wrinkled, bearded older man (**colour plate 13**). Some of his coins, even of his own independent reign, are up to the standard of Antoninus Pius, while others are down to that of his (actual) son Commodus.

(9) 180-92

During the reign of Commodus the amount of silver struck seems to drop; certainly rather scruffily produced silver coins became quite common. Bronze now describes all the non-bullion issues – perhaps rather kindly, since they all consisted of a mixture of copper and various extras such as tin, lead, and zinc. Many of the extra metals probably came from recycling old coin, and perhaps a portion of bronze scrap as well. The shape of the bronze coins was by this stage an irregular circle, usually with at least one straight edge, and sometimes several (**colour plate 8**). This may be the result of casting a row of blanks in a mould; they would be joined together as the liquid metal flowed along the row, and when cold would have to be separated by a chisel. The straight chisel cut could be hammered to make a curve, but was often left quite rough.

(10) 193-222

For the first time, this is a composite period made up of different (though linked) reigns. A lot happened to the coinage.

Some readers might find a gap between section 9, which covered the period until 192, and section 10, which starts in 193; but this break is illusionary, because Commodus was killed on the last day of 192. After a short, disreputable interval in which the Imperial Guard put the empire up for auction to the highest bidder, a war broke out which saw Septimius Severus victorious. He promised much to the army under his control; and when the battles were over the silver in the coinage was reduced. It seems very likely that the two facts are connected, but I have left them as independent just in case. There was certainly a military pay rise in denarii, and a drop in silver content to about 48%, and the two cancelled each other out. The drop in silver was not in any way as marked as it had been under Nero, but the news clearly leaked out.

Caracalla, the son of Septimius, produced a new silver coin in 214 (**colour plate 15**). It had a radiate crown on the emperor's head instead of the more usual laurel wreath, and weighed about half as much again as the denarius. The two coins were struck side by side, in the same 48% silver. The radiate crown had been used to differentiate the dupondius, worth two asses, from the as which had a laureate portrait; using this reasoning some people think the radiate piece is a double denarius, although if we take a practical view it is a 1.5 denarius. Kevin Butcher (now based in Beirut) points out that for the first time the western provinces are striking a coin with the same silver content as some of the eastern mints (which have not yet been mentioned), such as Antioch. He asks whether the West is coming into line with the East, but usually gets a rather rough reply from ancient historians based textually, temperamentally, and even physically in the Roman West.

Caracalla gives himself the name Antoninus Pius (see phase 7 above), as does the last emperor in this phase, Elagabalus, who reigned from 218-22. These other two emperors also both struck the radiate silver coin: but this went out of fashion for a time in the next phase.

(11) 222-38

Severus Alexander, who became emperor in 222, was related to the family of Septimius Severus, and reigned until 235. Maximinus was in power for the next three years. The denarius, which by now was nearly 450 years old, gave its last breath in this phase (this is however only strictly true if we take it as a solid piece of metal – as a unit of account it continued for well over another 150 years).

The silver standard continued to decline, and the bronze coinage became more and more mixed in metal and irregular in shape; however, every so often perfect coins were produced. Thus while straight-sided sestertii are most unlikely to belong to the first century AD, perfectly round coins were sometimes still being produced in the middle of the third century AD (**43**).

(12) 238-60

The changes in the coinage during this phase become more important than the changes in Emperor, and this is true up to the end of the fourth century, and beyond. There were at least fifteen emperors between 238 and 260; some tallies, depending on whether you include sons and usurpers, would be higher. Gallienus, who came to the throne with his father Valerian in 253, was still there after 260, though Valerian was in captivity in Persia after 259.

The date of 260 is chosen for the end of the phase because it forms a notional borderline between radiate coins which appear silvery, and others which look like copper (**colour plate 21**). The silver content sank from 238 onwards, and was probably down to about 5-8% by 260. This lowering of the intrinsic value of the coins must have led to a lowering of purchasing power, and this in turn made the large scale production of bronze less and less economic.

While the historical sequence is complicated, the coin sequence is fairly simple. Low silver radiates were struck in great numbers, bronze became less used, and even gold started to vary in both weight and fineness (**colour plate 18**). Whether the gold denomination, the aureus, was toppled is hotly debated: most of the rather uncommon gold coins have widely differing weights, so it is almost a matter of guesswork to judge what the notional weight of a notional aureus might be. I assume that gold came to be exchanged by weight, but this is not completely agreed.

(13) 260-75

The reign of Gallienus continued until 268. By this date the radiate seldom contained as much as 2% silver, striking of bronze had almost stopped, and gold was variable. The radiate might once have been a double denarius, but now it had sunk to the purchasing power of a small copper coin of the reign of Augustus. The only other coin commonly minted was rather variable gold, while a random selection of old copper coins were still in circulation to some extent. Whatever was happening in the economic field in theory, the actual day-to-day coinage

6 *Postumus (260-8) struck a number of sestertii on newly made blanks, but also used up old and worn sestertii – here that of Hadrian (117-38). The radiate crown imposed on the sestertius may have doubled its value*

7 *Radiate of Postumus (260-8). The legend has become set for every emperor beginning IMP C, then the name, then PFAVG. At the top of the F on this coin there is a blob of metal which suggests that a small piece had broken out of the die*

was in a mess. This does not necessarily mean that the economy was in turmoil or had collapsed – for example large-scale inflation only seems to have hit Egypt in the next phase, although it is tempting to regard this as a separate story. This leads directly to the very valid question of how far can you have (or did you have) differences of situation within one supposedly united empire?

Part of the answer in this phase is that the empire between 260-75 was not united. In the eastern deserts Queen Zenobia took over Palmyra before she was brought to heel. In quite different conditions a series of at least three major names, Postumus, Victorinus and Tetricus, took over the Gallic Empire, which depended on large cities like Cologne, Trier and Lyon, and seems to have included most of north-west Europe, including Britain and reaching down to Spain (**6 & 7, colour plate 19**). An examination of the Gallic empire through the distribution of its coins is a subject ripe for research; but as these coins seem always to have been a bit finer, year by year, than those of the central empire based in Rome, it is very difficult to distinguish political limits to circulation due to the sensible desire to use the most valuable coin available.

(14) 275-94, or 295, or 296

This title should suggest caution (or simply perhaps that I don't know what I am talking about). But there is an enormous change in Roman coinage between 294-6, and it happens in different places at different times. The story in fact goes back to 274 when the emperor Aurelian, after mopping up the opposition, turned his attention to really important things like the money supply (**8**). The coinage of the early part of his reign belongs totally with the period which preceded his succession – it is nasty, base, and scruffy. Then, around 274, he reformed the coinage. 'Reform' is always a difficult word because you have to ask who benefited, since it suggests that matters improved. Or perhaps people in the early twenty-first century are cynical enough to think that most of the reforms they have lived through have been nothing more than rearrangements of differing depth, aimed mainly at saving money for the state, handing out money to the select few, and saving administrators trouble.

This is the light in which to view Aurelian's reform, in which he discontinued the small copper radiates and substituted a larger, better-struck radiate coin with over 4% silver in it. The coin looked good, and it simplified the paying of state bills in that one new radiate probably equalled a small bag of old radiates; but to the person in the market this spelled disaster. The scruffy

8 *This radiate of Aurelian (270-5) shows a larger, better struck coin than those produced from 260-73. Aurelian's reform of 273-4 also raised the amount of silver in the coins*

old radiate was perfect for dashing out to the stalls to make a few quick purchases – a cabbage, three eggs, and a piece of cheese. The new radiate left you, in modern terms, with no change smaller than a one pound (or dollar or euro) coin, and that makes simple shopping difficult. The coin had the signs XXI on the lowest part of the reverse (the exergue). This could be XX = 20 and I = 1, or it could be XXI = 21. But 20 of what to one of what, or 21 what? One French professor, in uncharacteristically light-hearted mood, once wrote an article giving 21 explanations for the signs XXI. The best guess – and it is only a guess – is that it means I part of silver in XX parts of copper, since the silver content goes towards, but never reaches, 5%.

This radiate, supported by much better-controlled and struck gold (**colour plate 22**), makes up the coinage from 274 to the Great Reform which started in 294. By this time it is possible to see the mint organisation changing drastically. New mints, or branches of the Rome original, had started up throughout the third century. Sometimes they were rebel mints like Cologne or Trier, which were kept working when official rule was restored; in other cases they were new branches sited nearer to the frontiers and so the garrison soldiers who probably absorbed a large part of mint output (for instance Milan and/or the Balkans in the 250s). Sometimes production which looked similar to Rome, but with clear differences, was established in old eastern mints such as Antioch. The idea that Rome could produce all the coinage needed by the western empire was on the way out, and was totally killed off after 294.

There is one loose end, and that of course is in Britain. Just as the Gallic Empire had been divided from the central Empire from 260-74, so Britain was separated from 286-96. Under the emperors Carausius and Allectus Britain struck its own coins for the first time, produced better silver than the Central Empire, and generally seems to have survived well. This will form part of a later chapter; for the moment all that we need to note is that Britain was not available to take part in Diocletian's Great Reform until after the death of Allectus in 296. Then Britain returned into line.

The East from Augustus to 294

In a sense the coinage which circulated around the eastern half of the Mediterranean area is not directly relevant to Britain. For many years it was a subject very difficult to understand, or even to read about; then David Sear published his one volume summary of Greek Imperial Coins. Now a monumental work is in progress, led by Andrew Burnett in the British Museum and Michel Amandry in Paris, to list, document, and comment on all Roman Provincial Coins. The first volumes have been published, and others are in active preparation. What follows is a view from Britain, and therefore highly partial and totally unbalanced.

As a very rough guide coins were first used in Asia Minor before 600 BC, in Sicily and South Italy in the early 500s, and even in Etruria by the 400s BC – but not in Rome until nearly 300 BC. When Augustus became the first emperor the Roman state had already expanded outside Italy, and virtually all the places they took over had their own coinage in place. Policy differed from place to place as to whether Roman coins were introduced, or the local mints were encouraged to produce coins on the Roman model, or these mints were left to their own devices – a case of it isn't broken, and it doesn't cost us anything, and there is no great propaganda gain to be had, so don't fix it.

This left hundreds of cities, once independent states, striking their own coins with a combination of types they had chosen sometimes centuries before, and very variable portraits of emperors who they had never seen. The striking of city gold was unusual by the first century BC – kings and kingdoms had seen to that, and Rome saw to the kingdoms. Silver was struck but was gradually discouraged. Since the city presumably had to finance the striking of its own coinage, and the Roman state had flooded the market with silver coins whose intrinsic silver value was not much different from the buying power or face value, there was little profit to be made. Thus there was little point in doing it and discouragement was probably not needed. Certainly by the late second century only a few cities or provinces struck silver coins, although bronze and copper coins were struck in profusion.

These coins rarely reach Britain, but if I needed a reason to mention them one is provided by an example which I recently tried to identify – and failed (after 40 years working with Roman coins, and 30 teaching about them, this was very good for me). By following all my own rules I narrowed it down to a bracket of about 40 years – which is good enough for any archaeologist – but the name of the emperor was corroded and the reverse showed just PROVINC. One e-mail appeal to the East, in fact to Beirut, gave me a lead, and David Sear's book did the rest. It was a coin for PROVINCIA DACIA, the province of Dacia, now a part of the NE Balkans, struck by the emperor Aemilian around 250. I mention this because it may happen to anyone and is a reminder that you have to keep the East in mind, even in Roman Britain.

A second reason for mentioning this is as an example of the way that issues in the third century were coming closer together. Ordinary cities used Greek for their coinage, just as they did for their shopping. High-ranking cities in the east switched to Latin legends when they rose to the rank of colonia, and their coinage often moved closer to that produced at Rome. Every so often the Rome mint had struck coins for places, provinces, or cities in the east and sent the whole consignment off to Antioch, Cyprus or wherever. This means that some coins which circulated mainly in the east look very western, like my Provincia Dacia coin.

One final point of hard finance. Most of the eastern cities that did strike silver did so on a different standard to Rome, the majority being lower in silver; but a few produced coins not only of a similar silver content, but also roughly the same size as the Roman denarius. This accounts for the fact that in large hoards of denarii from Britain you do get the occasional odd silver coin which comes from Lycia and Caesaraea in Cappadocia, both in Asia Minor, and Cyrene (**colour plate 7**) in the east of modern Libya. The great mint at Antioch used its own system, with which the western system did not mesh well until Rome changed in 214.

The great exception to almost everything is Egypt. This is extremely annoying because it is the one place where we have a good record of the lives of Everyday Country Folk, from laundry lists through marriage contracts to devious practices in army administration, preserved on papyrus together with good evidence on prices, coins, and their use. The annoyance comes from the fact that until the Great Reform of 294 Egypt has its own economic system and coin production, so we never know how far this evidence can be applied to the rest of the Empire.

Egypt retained the coinage it used from the last years BC, the coinage of the Ptolemies and the Cleopatras, and the mint of Alexandria produced copper drachmas, fractions, and four drachma pieces, the tetradrachm (**39**). This was notionally the same as the denarius; but, although it was heavier, it contained far less silver, and the result was coin that no one in their right mind would take to the west and try to use in a market. If you went to Egypt with good silver denarii you had to change them into tetradrachms – that may have caused friction. When you left the country Erik Christiansen says that you had to change your tetradrachms back into denarii: I maintain, possibly in the face of evidence, that compulsion would not be needed. Whatever the truth of this we can go very provincial and say that as far as Britain in the Roman period was concerned base silver tetradrachms never reached this far. Christiansen has looked at all the hoards of tetradrachms minted in Alexandria that he could find. The majority were clearly found in Egypt, and most of those now recorded as finds outside the country have a serious question mark against their real find spot.

This aside about Roman coinage *not* found in Britain is rather important for the discussion of coins that *are* found there. One or two copper coins from Alexandria have been found in excavations of Roman period sites in Britain; but this has never happened for a base silver tetradrachm. Yet one of the old coins most commonly taken into museums or to the field liaison officers of the Portable Antiquities Scheme for identification is the Alexandrian tetradrachm of the years 250-94. To cut a long story short, this is better evidence for the number of British soldiers who have served in the Sudan, the Western Desert, Suez, and Egypt itself than for any trade links between Roman Egypt and Roman Britain. When a few such coins are found in actual excavations in undisturbed layers I might change my view a little, but until then I do not believe they have anything to do with Roman Britain.

The changes in the western coinage detailed above for the years 222-74 left us with poor radiate coins and variable gold, and similar changes occurred in the East. Radiate coins were struck in places like Antioch, which continued its city and provincial coinages at the same time; but a double denarius (if it was that) with the purchasing power of a small copper coin obviously spelled the doom of copper and bronze in the East as well as the West, and the city coinages which relied on coin in these metals were in difficulties in the later third century. Few cities wanted to pay for the minting of copper coins around 260 when they cost more to produce than they were worth. By the 280s, apart from Alexandria and Antioch, eastern, that is Greek, coinage was all but extinct.

The Roman Empire from 294 to after 400

(15) 294-317: the Great Reform

Starting in 294, major changes hit the coinage. Greek disappeared from the coinage even of mints like Antioch and Alexandria. The portraiture of the emperors changed dramatically; at that time there were four emperors, two greater and two lesser, and instead of portraying individual features the coins suddenly depict four almost indistinguishable representations of The Emperor. Gold, which had varied substantially in the middle of the century, was well struck to a standard rate of 60 coins to the pound of good quality metal. Good silver had not been seen since the middle of the second century, except under Carausius (286-93) in Britain, but such coins suddenly appeared, and some were marked XCVI – 96 to the pound of silver. Three silvered bronze coins were struck. One type continued the idea of the radiate and it was accompanied by a larger and a smaller coin each with a laureate portrait (**colour plates 25-8**).

But the greater surprise comes in the total cessation of the local issues of the East, the end of the Greek mints at Antioch and Alexandria, and the subservience of all the new mints to the Central Plan. All struck the same coins at the same time, with the occasional lapse, and they differed only in the mint-mark. The system took a little time to shake down, but by about 320 the main centres were London, Trier, Lyon, Arles, Aquileia, Rome, Siscia, Thessalonica, Heraclea, Nicaea, Cyzicus, Antioch, and Alexandria. In 326 London closed and Constantinople, in the city newly re-founded by Constantine I, opened.

We have one very unusual piece of evidence for the year 301, preserved on pieces of an inscription from Asia Minor. It tells us of a coin reform in which most of the coins in use at the time seem to have their values, expressed in denarii, doubled. Some coins are described as bicharacta; there is no agreement as to what this might mean. I would like it to mean that the coins were of two metals (silver and copper) and so had two values, intrinsic value due to silver, and purchasing power decreed by the state. This is probably wishful thinking.

According to one interpretation of this Edict we could have after 301 silvered bronze coins of 2, 5, and 25 denarii; a silver coin of 100 denarii; and a gold coin of 1200 denarii. This is worth mentioning because there is another Edict of the year 301, the Edict on Maximum Prices, which gives quite remarkable details on a whole array of goods, maximum prices and wages, so that for a very short time we can construct a weekly set of household accounts for a sewer cleaner or camel driver. These people were paid 25 denarii a day, the lowest rate mentioned, probably the largest silver-copper coin, and a shopping list can be compiled to help spend say 100 denarii out of the weekly wage.

I say 'for a short time' because even within the 23 years of this period the coinage changed substantially and prices continued to rise as they had done for at least the past 50 years. The good silver of around 300 had, by about 315, sunk to very rare, coppery coin, and it soon died out. The large silver-copper coin dropped in size from about 10 to about 4g. The smaller silver-copper coins died out; gold was reformed to 72 coins to the libra (pound of twelve ounces, about 327g). It is probably pointless to ask for names for individual coins, or even how the different issues relate to one another. Perhaps the best thing to do is what most people in the markets had to do: accept coins as coins and assume a constant face value, but steadily diminishing purchasing power.

(16) 317-30. Settling down

Think back a moment to the 130s and 140s. Everything then went by emperor – the coins were of Trajan or Hadrian or Antoninus – and they changed when the emperor changed. Now in the early years of the fourth century the changes in coinage and changes in emperor have come adrift. Since we are following the coinage, the emperor has almost become expendable; and this comes through in the portraiture as well, where the image is that of The Emperor, rather the person with a personal name and a small chin or large nose.

At this period the emperor is Constantine and he is in the process of clearing up the competition left from the system of rule by the four emperors (tetrarchy) which ran from 293-306. The main date in fulfilling this aim was 324, when the last competitor was eliminated and his own family provided the only rulers of the empire; however, the coinage did not change in 324, but in 317 and 330.

By 317 the attempts at silver coinage, so promising around 300, had more or less run down. In 327 new silver of high standard was re-introduced, and this time it remained in circulation to the end of the empire with very little fluctuation in quality. Quantity however was very low – these coins are extremely rare now, and were probably never very common even when they were being struck and issued. This leaves gold, which had changed gradually to 72 coins to the libra (pound), and one silver-copper coin whose weight, silver content, and therefore face value and purchasing power, changed often and, to most of us, perplexingly. There are some people who think they know what was happening, but I am not yet convinced and I suggest simply noting that 'the coin' was not yet stable.

In 317 young members of the families of Constantine and competitor Licinius were made Caesars, assistant emperors, and this helps us to keep a check on the date. Types and mint-marks that they share must be after this 317, but if they are not shared by the next Caesars to be appointed (323) they must be before then. The design of the coins changed in that the most common type – of the sun god Sol standing holding a whip and a globe – disappeared. The sun had been the state choice of chief deity since the 270s, but after 312 Constantine had become involved with the Christian church, so later types were less obviously pagan (**colour plate 29**).

The end date on 330 for this period marks the time of the consecration of the New Rome, Constantine-city, or Constantino-polis (in Greek); but the coins for this belong to the next period.

(17) 330-48

The dedication of Constantinople in 330 demanded an issue of coins, and these were struck showing Constantinopolis holding a shield and sceptre, with a foot on a ship's prow to show the placing of the city on a vital sea-way (**colour plate 32**). Clearly however Old Rome had to be mentioned as well; so an equal issue of Urbs Roma was struck, with the time-honoured Wolf and twins (**9**). The issues, which continued till 335, were augmented with coins showing the Glory of the Army (Gloria Exercitus), with two soldiers each

9 *After the Dedication of Constantinople in 330 Old Rome needed an issue of coins to prevent rivalry. This issue was struck for VRBS ROMA, and is the reverse showing the Wolf and Twins with the mint and batch mark TRP – Mint of Trier, first workshop*

■

10 *The standard issue for the years 330-5, rather like the basic postage stamps which run through all those special issues, shows two soldiers with two military standards between them. The legend celebrates the GLORIA EXERCITVS, the glory of the army. The two standards belong only to the years 330-5: another example of the reverse dating the coin, rather than the emperor doing so. Mint mark TR P, as before (see* **9***), but a different period of striking because the dot is in a different place* ■

holding a military standard, a spear and a shield (**10**). These are probably the most common Roman coins ever struck, though their distribution does vary from place to place.

In 335 the coins got smaller, the two soldiers now held one standard (**colour plate 33**), and Urbs Roma and Constantinopolis were struck much less often. The change in design from two standards to one might simply be due to the reduction in size of the coin; on the other hand it might have some cosmic significance, but if so we know nothing about it. In 337 Constantine the Great died. His sons first eliminated all their nearest and dearest who might have got in the way before announcing the death, then set to squabbling among themselves. In 340 the eldest son, Constantine II was killed. In 341, or thereabouts, the coins with soldiers and the last few Rome and Constantinople issues stopped – a good demonstration of the total lack of connection between changes in emperors and changes in coins.

As far as we can see at present, the mints did not strike coins continuously. The sort of evidence available comes from the mint-marks found on each coin under the reverse type; below the ground, for instance, on which the wolf of the 'Wolf and Twins' type is standing. Coins from Trier always had TR, and to this was added the workshop number, P(rimus) = first, or S(ecundus). This gave either PTR or TRP. A whole range of symbols could then be added, so different batches had TRP dot, or TRP dot in crescent, or TRP palm branch. These mint-marks can be dated in a loose way by the princes on whose coins they appear: so for example a mint-mark shared by Constantine I, Constantine II and Constantius II, but not by Constans, belongs after 330 but before 333 (when Constans became a Caesar).

Likewise, marks for the four princes, but not Delmatius, belong to before 335, when he became Caesar. At Arles, Delmatius *et al.* have two mint-marks before the coins drop in size, and the two soldiers only have room to hold one standard, while at Trier and Lyon there are no two soldier and two standard coins for Delmatius; he starts with the one standard issues. There is therefore a phase at the end of 335 when Arles is striking copper coins, but Lyon and Trier are not. These examples could be multiplied considerably. Production was not continuous, but we do not know what caused it to start or to stop.

The western mints seem to have closed down, at least for the production of silver-copper, between about 341-6. The eastern mints appear to be striking in this material around 343 because the emperor in the East, Constantius II, commemorated his twentieth anniversary: VOT / XX / MVLT / XXX, the vows (vota) undertaken for twenty years (XX) have been completed, now more (multa) are undertaken looking forward to the thirtieth (XXX) anniversary (**colour plate 39**). This, in a sense, was unsporting. The emperor in the West, Constans, only became Caesar in 333, so if he had struck coins at the same time he would have had to admit that he was the little brother by ten years, with the legend VOT / X / MVLT / XX. He wisely avoided this propaganda disaster, striking no coins for a time, then about 346 started an issue to commemorate the victories of our lords and emperors: Victoriae DD Augg Q NN. Two letters indicate two people: thus this pays homage to The Victories Dominorum (of the Lords, two of them) Augustorum (of the emperors, two of them) que (and) Nostrorum (ours - both of them) (**colour plate 38**).

This is one clear instance when the notion of a single coinage over the whole empire wore a little thin. Gold and silver continued to be very rare. Everything then changed in the year of the eleven hundredth birthday.

(18) 348-64. The Birthday and end of Constantine's family

Rome was 1100 in AD 348. Constantine's youngest son Constans was killed in 350; the remaining son, Constantius II, died in 361, and the last of the family Julian, a step-great-nephew, was killed in Persia in 363. The changing emperors posed no problems for the coinage, but the Birthday was rather a challenge. When Rome was founded two legends grew up, one Etruscan and one Latin. A number of birds were seen, omens were clear, but different; to the Etruscans there would be 11 ages (saecula, of 110 years each) of Rome, while the Latins foresaw 12 ages each of 100 years. For the first time in a thousand years the two systems coincided to spell quite clearly the Beginning of the End. Ten Etruscan saecula had passed, 1100 years, only 110 years to go; and eleven Latin centuries had gone by, leaving 100 more years. So the End was slightly hazy; but it still posed an image and communication problem.

In 248 there had been expensive games to celebrate the Millennium, and the emperor of the time, Philip, commemorated the events on his coins with a series of animals shown in the circus (**colour plate 36**). 348 was a time for more reflective rejoicing. The advisors surpassed themselves and produced an

11 *Around the year 357 gold coinage suddenly reappeared in more common use. This issue of Constantius II uses the three-quarter facing bust which had not been commonly used before; it had been tried out by Postumus (260-8) in the Gallic empire, but is not very practical because the features of the face tend to wear rather quickly*

anniversary whose main symbol, on coins at least, was the Phoenix and the motto Fel Temp Reparatio – The happiness of former times has returned (**40**). Things are going well; yes, the ages are moving on, but Rome is like the Phoenix, she will come to a formal end only to rise immediately from the ashes. The coinage system was itself reformed with several concurrent denominations – larger and smaller coins in some sort of relationship to one another – but the basic coin was still copper-silver, and gold and silver continued to be rare.

Then in about 357 a change as great as that of Diocletian's time took place: the silver-copper lost its silver, if not in 357 then certainly by 363, and silver coinage was again struck in large numbers. Gold also suddenly becomes less rare in the surviving record (**11**). Very little has been made of this change, but I think it is extremely important. I would especially like to know the effect of the change on the rate of inflation; but that is work for future research.

The official emperors were supplemented by usurpers in Gaul (Magnentius and Decentius) and the Balkans (Vetriano), and after the dynasty of Constantine ended with the death of Julian in 363 it was very quickly replaced by the Dynasty of Valentinian, which lasted well into the fifth century.

(19) 364-78. The last phase of togetherness

The reign of Valentinian I (died 375) and his brother Valens (died 378) is one of the most uniform in the history of the empire. To some people this would make it boring; to others it is a chance to set aside the complications of what types appeared when and where and to focus on the production and distribution of imperial coinage.

12 *The copper issues from 364 onwards were free of all added silver for the first time for over a century. For the years 364-78 there are only two common types for the emperors Valentinian I (364-75), Valens (364-78) and Gratian (367-83). This is a third reverse which was only issued at Arles for Gratian, showing him as the GLORIA NOVI SAECVLI – the glory of the new age. The N to the left of the figure is a batch mark and not part of the design*

After an initial settling down period the bronze coinage, by now emptied of any silver content, showed two main reverse types. On one the emperor walks to the right carrying a military standard with the chi-ro, the first two letters of the name of Christ in Greek, and dragging after him a kneeling prisoner; the legend was GLORIA ROMANORVM, the glory of the Romans. The second type showed Victory walking to the left holding up a wreath; the legend here said that victory provided the SECVRITAS REIPVBLICAE, the safety of the state (**colour plate 40**). There was one more type which was fairly common in the West, and was struck only at the mint of Arles and only for the young son of Valentinian, Gratian. He became joint, but junior, emperor in 367 and his special issue lasted until the death of his father in 375. The reverse proclaimed GLORIA NOVI SAECVLI, the glory of the new age, and showed the emperor face-on holding a standard and shield (**12**). Gratian's junior status can be seen on the obverse of the coin by the way the lettering goes right the way round without a break; for senior emperors there is a break after the letters DN VALEN for the top of the portrait, and then SPFAVG. At this date all the legends are the same except for individual names; D(ominus) N(oster) so-and-so P(ius) F(elix) AVG(ustus) – our lord so-and-so the right thinking, fortunate, emperor.

Silver coins continued to be produced in reasonable numbers, and to circulate to some extent. During the reign they acquired the letters PS (pusulatum, refined silver) which was added to the mint-mark on the bottom of the reverse (exergue) (**13, colour plate 42**). Thus a coin of Trier might

1 *The main coins of the period AD 1 to 400 shown at twice their actual size. (a) Brass sestertius of Trajan (98-117). (b) Copper as of Antoninus Pius (138-61). (c) Silver denarius of Marcus Aurelius (161-80). (d) Reformed radiate coin of Probus (276-81). (e) Nummus or follis of Galerius (struck 294-305). (f) Silver-copper coin of the House of Constantine (struck 330-5). (g) Copper coin of the House of Valentinian (struck 364-78). (h) Copper coin of the House of Theodosius (struck 388-402)*

2 *Gold aureus of Claudius (41-54) showing the triumphal arch set up to commemorate the conquest of Britain. On the arch is the victorious emperor on horseback between two military trophies*

a

3 *Three very good copies of the as of Claudius I showing Minerva going right with spear and shield. Most Claudian copies are far below this standard*

b

c

4 *Perfect (museum) example of a denarius of Marc Antony struck in the East to mention all the legions attached to him in his final battle with Octavian/Augustus. Struck just before the battle of Actium in 31 BC in a partly debased silver, it shows a legionary eagle between two military standards. LEG VIII*

5 *An excavated example of* **4** *after two centuries of wear. The eagle can be seen left of the centre of the coin; the number of the legion has worn away*

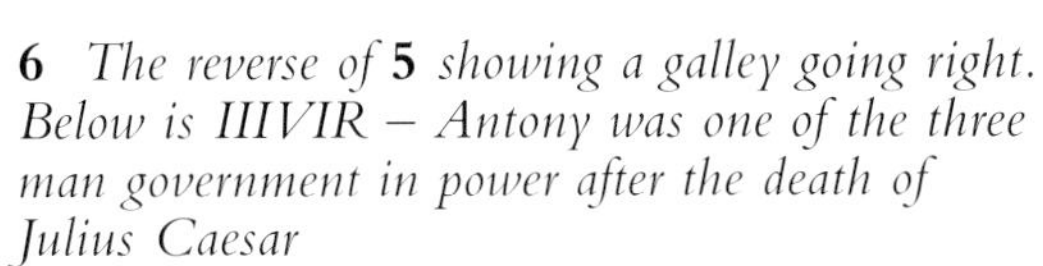

6 *The reverse of* **5** *showing a galley going right. Below is IIIVIR – Antony was one of the three man government in power after the death of Julius Caesar*

7 *Silver drachma of Trajan (98-117) minted in Cyrene in modern Libya. (Obverse) The legend is in Greek: NEP TPAIAN for the Latin NER(VA) TRAJAN. (Reverse) The head of Zeus Ammon, worshipped at Cyrene. The legend begins HMAPX – part of the Imperial titles. These drachmas circulated alongside the denarius*

8 *Sestertius of Commodus (180-92) commemorating Victories in Britain. Victory is sitting on a pile of captured arms, writing on a shield*

9 *Plated denarius of the Roman republic (56 BC). When first struck it would seem to be perfect, and only the experienced money-changer could 'see' the bronze through the silver plate*

10 *Plated denarius of Severus Alexander (222-35). There is nothing irregular about the design; when the silver plate was complete it would appear a legal coin*

11 *Two sets of two coins, all denarii of Augustus (around 19 BC) with a portrait facing right and the legend CAESAR AVGVSTVS. One pair consists of coins struck from the same die, the other pair, of two different coins. Decide which is which, and why*

12 *Two aurei of Faustina I, deceased wife of Antoninus Pius (struck around 150). For this pair of coins I find it more difficult to decide quickly whether or not they are from the same die*

13 *Two aurei of Marcus Aurelius: (a) about AD 155; (b) about 175. The two portraits of Marcus Aurelius (full emperor 161-80) show how the representation of one person can change through time. The first shows the young prince while his adoptive father (Antoninus) was still alive, the second Aurelius later in his own reign. There cannot be much more than 20 years between the two portraits*

14 *Denarius of Hadrian (117-38). He set the fashion in the second century of wearing a beard*

15 *(Left) Caracalla – a nickname for another Antoninus (196-217) – introduced the new silver radiate coin late in 214. It has been called an antoninianus (for fairly obvious reasons, a coin of Antoninus), but this is certainly wrong. Radiate is much simpler and is clearly correct as a description. Note that Antoninus calls himself Pius as part of his name, before his title, Augustus. The real Antoninus was Augustus first, then called Pius. The coin might be a double denarius, but is only one and a half times the weight. (Right) Denarius of Caracalla, struck in the same 50% silver-copper as the larger radiate*

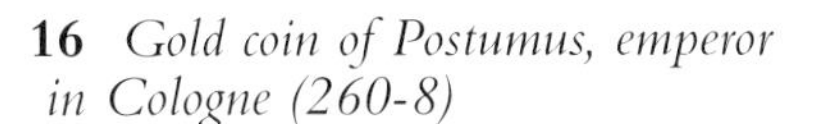

16 *Gold coin of Postumus, emperor in Cologne (260-8)*

17 *Gold coin of Gallienus, emperor in Rome (253-68). These two coins (***16** *and* **17***) were struck at roughly the same time, but Gallienus had all the resources of the Official Roman Empire, and Postumus only the break-away resources of the Gallic Empire centred in Cologne. From the preparation of the flan, the standard of the lettering, the size and weight of the coin you might have thought it the other way round*

18 *(a) & (b) Two gold coins of Gallienus (253-68) show that standards are slipping. The flans are thin and not well prepared, and neither coin is 100% gold: (a) looks silvery, (b), more coppery*

19 *Top: (left): Radiate of Postumus (260-8). Even on the copper coins of his reign the portraiture and lettering of Postumus are carefully engraved, but the flans on which the coins were struck were less well prepared; (right): Radiate of Victorinus (268-70). Victorinus has a recognisably individual portrait which distinguishes him from the other Gallic Emperors. Bottom: (left): Radiate of Tetricus I (270-4). The portrait of Tetricus is different yet again; (right): Radiate of Tetricus II (270-4), son of Tetricus I. All his coins show a young portrait. In the fourth century accurate representation of age becomes less and less common*

20 *Top: (left to right): Radiate of the deified Claudius II (after his death in 270) with the legend DIVO CLAVDIO. At this point the coinage sank to its lowest level in metal and production, yet the emperor is immediately recognisable; Barbarous radiate (270-90). After about 275 the radiate coins were copied. The portrait might be young, and the few letters which can be made out could include a T and an E, so this might be a copy of a coin of Tetricus II; Barbarous radiate, and there is little more that can be said about it. Lettering has vanished and portraiture has not been attempted. Bottom: (left to right): Radiate of Claudius II after his death in 270, showing the commemorative altar and the legend CONSECRATIO; Barbarous radiate copying the altar reverse of Claudius II. The design is sketchy, but the lettering is reasonable; Barbarous radiate again copying the altar reverse. The lettering has gone badly astray, but the altar is recognisable. The brassy metal and the type of corrosion suggest that this may have been made of a recycled brass sestertius*

21 *(Left): Base silver radiate of Gallienus (253-68) with a characteristic portrait. The coin might contain 15% silver but probably no more: yet it has a silvery appearance. (Right): Radiate of Claudius II (268-70) with a characteristic portrait and a silvery sheen. It is unlikely that there is as much as 3% silver in such a coin*

22 *Gold coin of Carinus and Numerian struck about 283. (Obverse): The two emperors are shown together. The flan is perfectly made, the lettering is excellent and the die-cutting accomplished: coinage is recovering from its mid-century lapse (see* **17***). (Reverse): Victory holding a military trophy goes right. The victory is of the two emperors jointly (VICTORIA AVGG). Gold coins of the third century are rare but this is an example found in Britain at Richborough. (Electrotype)*

23 *Sunday 18 April 1976 at Springhead in Kent; the first coins of a hoard of gold appear in the excavation.* Photograph: a colleague

24 *Copper, corroded, and not very appealing. The hoard from the basilica Aemilia in Rome, still in its linen bag as it was when burned in the sack of the city in August 410*

25 *The great reform of Diocletian around 294 includes new style gold with the minimalist portraits of the four co-emperors – here Maximian*

26 *New good silver (around 295), four years after Carausius managed it, simply says that XCVI (96) of these coins are struck from each pound of silver (quality control) at T, the mint of Ticinum (Pavia)*

27 *The silver bronze denominations of Diocletian's reform (from 294) start with the largest, the nummus, often called the follis. London's mint started off with unmarked issues, then the mint name appeared. GENIO POPVLI ROMANI, the Genius or Guardian Spirit of the Roman people, was the same design or type whether in Alexandria or London*

28 *In Diocletian's reform of 294 there were two smaller coins. (a) This is the larger one, the radiate. These are not common in Britain, but appear quite frequently in the Mediterranean area. (b) The smallest coins of 294 with a laureate head, perhaps worth two denarii, are rare everywhere*

29 *After 294 there was usually just one bronze denomination struck with some silver added, which might be called the nummus. (Obverse): This example is of Constantine the Great (about 322) wearing an ornate helmet. (Reverse): In the early fourth century the nummus declined in weight, size, and silver content. This shows an altar with the legend BEATA TRANQVILLITAS and belongs to the years 320-4. The mint is Trier and the coin was struck in the second workshop (STR). From now on the reverse type dates the coin much better than the portrait of the emperor*

30 *A youthful portrait of Constantius II, son of Constantine I, around 330. Constantine remained the only full emperor until his death, so Constantius is titled NOBC, the most noble Caesar (assistant emperor)*

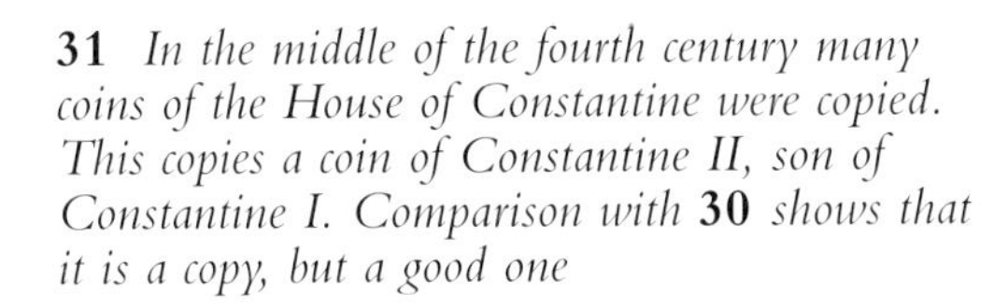

31 *In the middle of the fourth century many coins of the House of Constantine were copied. This copies a coin of Constantine II, son of Constantine I. Comparison with* **30** *shows that it is a copy, but a good one*

32 *(Left): Coins were struck for the Dedication of Constantinople the new capital in 330, and for the next five years. The City is shown as Victory with spear and shield and a foot on a prow – as the city was sited on the narrow straight between Europe and Asia. From the second workshop (B: greek 2) of the mint of Siscia. (Right): Constantinopolis coins were also copied in the middle of the fourth century. The design here is fair, and the engraver has copied the mint signature of Lyon (first workshop of Lugudunum PLG)*

33 *(Left): In 335 the coins which had shown two soldiers with two standards changed, as the coin got smaller, to show just one standard. The issue continued from 335-41. This is from the second workshop at Rome (R wreath S). (Right): The coins showing one standard were copied after about 340. The type is clearly identifiable, but the coin is smaller and the design is beginning to come apart*

34 *This looks at first sight a perfectly respectable 'One Standard issue' – though detailed examination shows some blunders. Does the head side (***35***) help?*

35 *Obverse of* **34**. *This shows the design of Roma and the legend Urbs Roma. The reverse should have been the typical Rome symbol of the Wolf and Twins. The mixing up (muling) of a head and a tail from different designs is common in the copies produced in the middle of the fourth century*

36 *After the 1100th anniversary of Rome had been celebrated in 348, the legend thought up for the occasion (Fel Temp Reparatio – the return of the happiness of former times) continues with issues showing a standing soldier leaning over to spear an enemy who has fallen off his horse – referred to in shorthand as Fallen Horseman. Mint-mark SMHB, Sacred Mint of Heraclea, second workshop*

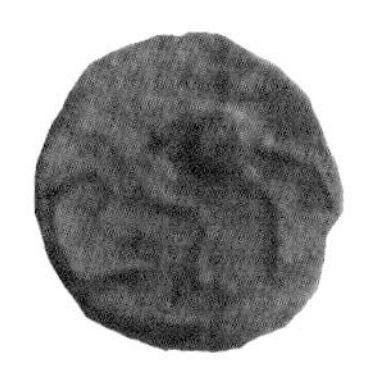

37 *The large Fallen Horseman coins were often copied in Britain, declining to a very low standard in all respects. This is a copy from the Lydney hoard with a diameter of about 3mm. At least the haunches of the fallen horse can be seen – if little else*

38 *About 345 the western mints struck an issue commemorating the victories of our lords the two emperors (DDAugg Q NN). Mint of Trier*

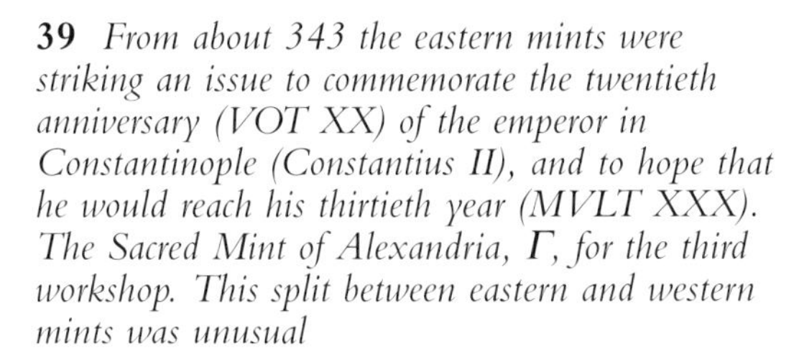

39 *From about 343 the eastern mints were striking an issue to commemorate the twentieth anniversary (VOT XX) of the emperor in Constantinople (Constantius II), and to hope that he would reach his thirtieth year (MVLT XXX). The Sacred Mint of Alexandria, Γ, for the third workshop. This split between eastern and western mints was unusual*

40 *Reverse of the House of Valentinian, commemorating Victories of the (Reipublicae) State – rather wishful thinking. The mint of Siscia, near the front line of fighting, was in high production with many different batch-marks. This is an example of one of the two of those mint-marks that arrive in Britain*

41 *(Left): A small copper coin of Magus Maximus (383-7) minted in Arles – then called Constantia. The city gateway is surrounded by the legend Spes Romanorum – the hope of the Romans. This small denomination is the only common coin of Maximus found in Britain. (Right): A larger copper coin of Magnus Maximus (383-7). The emperor raises (Reparatio) a kneeling Respublica (State), presumably after previous troubles have been overcome. This larger coin is commonly found in the Mediterranean region, but not in Britain*

42 *Good silver coinage comes into Britain again from 357, after a long period of absence. This was made of refined silver (PuSulatum) at the mint of Trier. The silver standard remains high (95%+) to the bitter end*

43 *Perfectly struck gold of high quality rarely got lost. (Obverse): This is a solidus of Arcadius (383-408). (Reverse): Around the emperor 'walking over' the enemy is a legend which says there were three emperors (AVGGG). It was struck by the Court Mint (COM) when based at Milan (MD) of refined gold (OB). (Electrotype of a coin found at Richborough)*

44 *The very last coins which turn up with any regularity in Britain are coins of Constantine III (408-11) who, like Magnus Maximus, started his career in Britain. Both silver and gold coins are very rare. This gold issue comes from Gaul*

13 *After the 360s the newly arrived, fairly common, silver coinage often guarantees its silver standard by adding the abbreviation PS to the mint-mark. Thus here, below the seated figure of Roma, TRPS – mint of TR(ier) PuSulatum, refined silver*

14 *Gold coins settled down in the late fourth century into an almost changeless mould, as did the portraits. The vital part for identification is the name VALENS between the inevitable beginning DN and end PF AVG. The emperor is usually unbearded and almost always wears a jewelled diadem*

say TRPS – mint of TR(ier), struck in refined silver. Gold continued to be struck at high quality, and quite early in the reign a new source of bullion seems to have been exploited. This is shown by small amounts of precious rare metals such as platinum and palladium in the gold, accidental contents which come from the new source of metal, and slipped through the refining process because their properties are very similar to those of gold (**14**). The equivalent to 'refined silver' was OB for Obryzium, refined gold. An extra addition to the information given was the abbreviation COM, stating that the gold was only struck in the mint of the Comitatus (roughly, the court) under the control of the COM(es) sacrarum largitionem (the Count of the Sacred Largesse – hand-outs) (**colour plate 43**). A mint-mark for Trier might then be TROB or TRCOM, or, later on, COMOB in the exergue and T and R on either side of the figure standing in the reverse. Finally, a new gold coin was struck in moderate quantities during the period; this was the tremis, or one-third of the solidus, the gold piece. John Kent always said that a new coin meant a new purpose, such as taxation or other state payment; but this has not yet been ascertained.

(20) 378-88. Diversity

After the very uniform period which ended in 378 some diversification seems to have been inevitable, and this struck in several different ways. Gold and silver continued a smooth course as before; but bronze changed, and instead of a single copper coin, two denominations were struck, one larger than the 364-78 coin, and one smaller (**colour plate 41**). The distribution of these coins also varies, with the north-west of the empire getting the smaller coins, and the Mediterranean region the larger ones. The types were not uniform at all mints and, even worse, different types were struck for varying lengths of time in different imperial spheres of authority. These were roughly East and West, but it is too early to talk of a split empire. This means that the periods which have been used so far to divide up the coinage throughout the empire now cease to work, as while there is agreement up to 383, after that year variety ensues. The date I have used to end the period, 388, passes almost unnoticed in the eastern mints.

(21) 388-408

Gold and silver continue their uniform course, while in copper variety prevails. The West produced large numbers of small coins, while the east continued with different denominations (**15 & 16**). In the previous period the variety showed differences of distribution between the NW and the Centre; now it is becoming more and more a question of the Eastern Mediterranean area and The Rest.

The idea of the denarius as an accounting unit is still floating about, but the more usual unit now is the nummus. Basically this translates as coin, but it is used as if it meant a value as well. There is no agreement as to whether the small coins of the West are nummi (plural of nummus) or 4 or 5 nummus pieces. For the NW provinces only these coins were available, and one of the few things known for certain is that to buy a gold piece you had to hand over 7200 nummi.

Using a (highly undesirable) mixture of laws of different dates, an interesting equation appears. You must pay 7200 bronze nummi for a gold solidus (AD 445). If a tax has been levied in bronze, you must pay in gold at the rate of one solidus for each 25 libra (pounds) of bronze expected (AD 396). The nummus weighs about 1.13g, so 7200 weigh 8136g. 25 libra of bronze at 327g for a libra come out at 8175g.

15 *The last copper coins to arrive in Britain both showed Victory – hardly an accurate piece of news. In this coin Victory walks left with a wreath held out in front of her. This type, VICTORIAE AVGGG, the victories of the three emperors, came from the mints of Trier, Lyon or Arles (388-402)*

16 *The other type of the last copper coins to enter Britain shows Victory dragging after her a captive: in front of her as part of the design is a chi-rho, the first two letters of the name of Christ in Greek. This type, SALVS REIPVBLICAE, came usually from the mints of Aqileia and Rome (388-402)*

Such speculation may be pointless, but it does underline the very important fact that the state was increasingly thinking in terms of bullion, and regarding copper and bronze coins as no more than lumps of struck metal. The state certified its issues as refined, whether gold or silver, yet when the tax collectors and officials had collected the one or two solidi from each person they wanted not a bag of coin, but a fused lump of certified pure gold of the right weight. Presumably there were sub-standard solidi around and, after bludgeoning each tax payer into paying with perfect coin, it was too easy for the officials further down the line to extract a few good coins and insert instead an equal number of false ones, something more difficult with a lump of solid gold, marked with its standard and weight. It almost suggests that the state is going off the messy idea of coinage.

Epilogue

As the western provinces changed managements, from Roman Imperial to New Kingdoms, so the copper coinage in the west shut down. The mints like Trier and Lyon produced few copper coins after about 402; Arles and Aquileia went on for a time, but then petered out. Rome itself never again struck a really large issue of copper after about 408. By the middle of the fifth century, the striking of copper coinage was more or less confined to the East of a notional net stretched from the south of Sicily, through Malta, to Cape Bon in Tunisia. That same net also seems to have stopped eastern coins moving west.

Silver ran down as the western sources in Spain and the Balkans changed hands; but gold has a fairly continuous history in both East and West. In the East the solidus of Constantine the Great continued as the basic gold coin with few changes into the full Byzantine empire, the Venetian ducat, and the coinage of the Knights of St John, and also had an influence on Islamic standards. In the West the New Kingdoms such as the Visigoths in France and Spain and the Ostrogoths in Italy continued to strike solidi and tremisses (thirds), and initially they struck under 'an imperial umbrella', using the representation and name of the current emperor, the reverse types and even the mint signatures, and leaving themselves off the coins completely. This either had a practical basis, enabling the coins to be accepted all over the Mediterranean area as the equals of the full Imperial versions, or it was an acknowledgement that the Emperor was still in some sense an overlord of the German kings, and that somehow gold and silver was still a part of the emperor's sacred person, and ought to be acknowledged as such.

When the Frankish and Lombard kings struck coinage in the sixth century they used their own names and concentrated on the third of the old solidus; but all over western Europe the coinage went off the use of gold before about 750, and the silver penny, denier or denarius took over.

2 Coinage in Roman Britain

In the first chapter I outlined the production of Roman coinage at an empire-wide level, with a bias towards the western provinces. Now it is time to home in on Britain in the Roman period, to look at what coinage was supplied and how Britain reacted to it. I shall leave a discussion of the evidence on which this is based until later. When I refer back to the first chapter I will simply put the phase number in brackets.

Up to AD 41 (or perhaps 64)

Finicky historians might object that the date used ought to be AD 43, when the Conquest of Britain by the forces of the emperor Claudius was completed. While I would consider their suggestions in the previous chapter, which was about the coins as struck, and depended heavily on written, that is historical, sources, I rule them out of order here.

There is absolutely no doubt that if Claudius came to the imperial throne in AD 41 coins struck with his name can date from any time between 41 and his death in 54; and I see no reason to question the historical date of 43 for the Claudian conquest. But when we talk about the date at which a coin was lost we are in the realms of archaeology (material studies), not history (documentary studies). As yet no archaeologist has produced a method for distinguishing rubbish pits filled in 41 and 42 or even early in 43 – that is, pre-conquest Claudian pits – from those filled after the conquest. If a rubbish pit had in its lowest, waterlogged, layers a wooden tablet with a letter from a soldier which should have been sent home to relations in Gaul, but got lost instead, saying 'After bringing the Britons to their knees the emperor has left for Rome . . . ' I would accept that the rubbish pit could not have been filled until after 43 at the earliest. But this would be historical (written) evidence, not archaeology.

A coin of Claudius in a rubbish pit is not the same as that letter. The letter states that the conquest has happened; the coin says only that Claudius is emperor, and relates nothing about events, for the reverse type of Minerva carrying a spear and shield may have no lettering at all. The letter gives an earliest date of 43, the coin gives an earliest date of 41; and either may have been lost much later than the date at which they were produced. At present it is a perfectly good possibility, though unlikely, that bronze coins of Claudius reached Britain before the invading armies of Claudius; but dating something like the conquest (a notion) by means of material remains (which do not have notions) is impossible.

If we are doubtful about the date of use and loss for coins of Claudius, which are marked with his name and titles and related to a good series of written sources, we must obviously be at sea over the British coinage which had certainly been produced for many years before the Claudian conquest.

I keep repeating Claudian and Conquest because there is much room for doubt. Julius Caesar firmly maintained that he had brought Britain into subjection to Rome in 55 and 54 BC, while Augustus claimed some sort of hold over people in Britain, if not the whole island. John Creighton has made out a good case for members of British noble families being educated in Rome in the years around AD 1, perhaps as Distinguished Hostages, and he sees a lot of Roman influence on the coinage these people produced when they returned to Britain after being incorporated into Mediterranean culture. He has asked whether there could be small units of Roman soldiers in Britain forming a bodyguard for such nobles before the reign of Claudius. It is important to stress that while he has only asked the question others, who are less wily, have enthusiastically replied 'There were Roman troops in Britain before the conquest'. The right answer, if there is one, to such a tempting question, is 'maybe'.

The British coinage cannot be summarised in a short space, it needs much more careful treatment. All that needs to be said for the present is that many people in parts of Britain before AD 43 knew perfectly well what coins were, and may have been accurately versed in their production and use. Coins were produced in gold, silver and bronze and copper, so a system of denominations vaguely similar to that of the Romans existed. They seem to have been struck until a date near to 43, and the question of continued production after that date is widely discussed, although the evidence at the moment for continued use is not very strong. On sites where the Roman overlies the British settlement, such as Silchester, British coins are found in Roman layers. Where the site of settlement shifts – such as the movement from the British settlement at Bagendon (Gloucestershire) to the Roman site three miles down the valley at Cirencester – there is little overlap of coins. Roman coins, if any, are rare at the British site; there are very few British coins among the thousands of Roman examples from the Roman site. Bagendon probably continued until the 60s AD; Corinium, the Roman Cirencester, may show activity from the 50s, but probably not before.

This is an important way of looking at the continued use of coin, and I shall use it again. Where there is continuity of occupation, the chances of turning up disused coins from earlier levels when a well or a rubbish pit is being dug are quite high. Where there are no earlier levels, there are no disused coins, and anything found belongs, at earliest, to the first levels of that site. This is not a matter of proof but of probability: I doubt if there is such a thing as positive proof in archaeology other than a statement that 'This was found there'. What the continued use of British coins in Roman times means is a matter of interpretation; and while interpretations can be disproved or falsified, I suspect they cannot be proved. For instance, the difference between the evidence at Silchester and Cirencester might be the difference between Silchester and Cirencester: coin use in the two places may well vary and this produces varying evidence. Alternatively, coin use may be the same, and the difference of evidence may be due to the shifting of occupation. I prefer the second alternative, both because it seems to work when applied to more places than just Silchester and Cirencester, and because at present it remains unfalsified as far as I know.

Again, this is not a matter of Death and Destruction – an edict on the day after the conquest forbidding the use of British coinage in this Brave New World. There is little need for such draconian measures. When the first tribute is levied, and some homely rural natives turn up with British coins in hand you just sneer at them; they soon learn.

But if these matters can be quite simply settled there is a major problem. If as 'Purveyor of Classic Mead to the noble Briton Covdob' you are quite happy to have soldiers from a nearby fort drinking in your establishment, you may be even happier when they pay in silver; but what do you give in change? The soldiers have silver as their pay because taxes were collected in old silver coin in Gaul and Spain to finance the army. As the mint is not striking copper at the moment (phase 2-3), and there is no mechanism for recouping old copper such as the asses of Augustus, they cannot give you the exact sum, which is much less than a silver denarius. They will not use British coins and they will not accept British coins as change. Some small change has to be produced from somewhere to make payment possible.

You can keep a reckoning of the drinks had by other villagers and you can settle up in different ways each month – one pays his bill in fresh eggs, another in milk, and yet another with a joint of lamb. But soldiers? They soon make some small change and bring it with them, and since they use it, it must be acceptable. These are the first efforts at what was to become a habit in Britain, the copying of official coins. Anyone used to coins in the City of Rome itself would have looked askance at these products, for they are smaller than the originals, far less well-prepared as blanks, often engraved in rather scrappy fashion and with lettering that is either incompetent or illiterate. But they usually copy the as in the correct copper, and the occasional dupondius in brass (**colour plate 3**).

Argument continues about the status of these Claudian Copies. An early theory claimed that the Romans used proper coinage, and the Britons copied it. This will certainly not work. Not only are genuine, mint of Rome coins very rare indeed in Britain, but the majority of the copies are found on military sites, and are scarce in the less Romanised areas which are probably British.

Robert Kenyon wrote a thesis on these coins, and was able to show how they developed particularly at Colchester, where there were several well-defined phases of occupation before 64, and at other sites in the backwoods of Britain which were not heavily militarised until the fifties and sixties AD. The weight and the workmanship declined in roughly five-year periods, by stages rather than by a continuous slide, as if the standards were being officially reduced.

Kenyon starting working on these copies while an art teacher, because he was interested in the artistic mechanics by which someone set out to copy a formal Roman design. Did the physical process account in part for the differences between the copy and the original? In part this was clearly true. The first thing the copier has to work out is that the design cut has to be the mirror image of the original. If it is a standing human figure few people will worry if it comes out the wrong way: even the head of the emperor sometimes faces left (although more often right). But many letters can only be depicted one way round. Every original coin showing Minerva with a spear and shield has an S to the left and a C to the right (SC – by decree of the Senate). C is fairly easy to reverse, but S is much more difficult, and not every copier managed it.

Another interesting point emerged when Robert tried the process out for himself. He had thought that the skilful part was the artistic task, the engraving of the die, and that the casting of blanks was just a chore; but the artist was brought to heel. With a few borrowed tools and some metals to cut into he produced some quite passable dies in a matter of hours; any Roman copier would have found them acceptable and given him a job at once. But he never really mastered casting blanks, even after some unexpectedly dangerous experiments. The problem lies in the high melting point of copper, which necessitates both bright red heat, and great care. Pouring the molten copper into cold moulds is difficult even when the moulds are completely dry, and if the moulds are warm or hot, the copper still might have cooled down before it has run into every corner. The shape of the blank creates more complications. If it is flat, the die has an impossible job to do; when the die is hit down by a hammer the metal of the blank has to be deformed into the ins and outs of the engraved die. This makes a deeply engraved die and a flat blank simply incompatible. A shallow die and a rounded blank give hope of success – if you can master the running of molten copper into a series of moulds.

The word 'official' has to be used at some point in relation to these copies because of the heavy army involvement, but it provokes a variety of reactions. Some thoroughly dislike the term and firmly maintain that the state would never tolerate, never mind sanction, such procedures. Others go for a compromise, and the adjective semi-official, which is so indefinable that I cannot see much use in it. I think I favour the idea of official approval being granted in view of 'special circumstances'. I also wonder whether the old privilege of the Imperator to strike coins for his army when out on campaign far from the

Rome mint had been totally forgotten. Under the Republic the Imperator (Commander-in-chief) wrote back to the Senate and asked for permission, and on the coins struck – which I think were always silver denarii – he put something approximating to IMPERAT EX SC, struck by the Imperator by decree of the Senate. Since the copies in Britain are overwhelmingly copper, there are no major problems of a legal nature; and similar examples also exist in Germany, where matching supply problems were felt, and in Spain where the closure of the surviving city mints by Claudius caused a lack of small change.

Since Nero seems to have avoided any large-scale striking of bronze in the first ten years of his succession (54-64, phase 3), this whole saga continues into his reign from that of Claudius. This gets the military addicts very upset, something I strongly approve of and enjoy: they are all historians rather than archaeologists, as is quite clear from the fact that they want dates in years, thus showing a basic lack of understanding of how archaeological reasoning works. The only written evidence on a site is usually the lettering on any coins found. Those discovered on sites occupied between 41 and 64 will either be earlier issues whose dates are irrelevant, coins of Claudius struck before about 47, or copies of these. If none of Nero's prolific issues is found then it might be fair to say that the site probably came to an end before about 70. In other words, archaeology in the form of coins can give a date range of 41 to 70, but cannot specify much more exactly. Archaeology in the form of pottery might suggest that Tiberio-Claudian samian pottery (*c*.30-50) is more common on the site than any other, thus dating occupation earlier in the coin bracket rather than later. It may on the other hand reveal that Neronian samian pottery (*c*.50 to 70) is present in reasonable amounts, so possibly putting the date later rather than earlier. But no archaeologists in their right minds (and I am afraid in this area of the subject many are not) would try to date a site to 'the military campaigns of 47' rather than 'the military campaigns of 56'.

Not only has the date of 43 dropped out of view, but now 54 as well. Let us just say 'earlier or later in the period 30-70', and hope that a few very diagnostic pottery sherds will push dating one way or another.

64-70: a short interlude

Soon after 64 the large issues of Nero's coins from mints in Rome and Lyon arrived in Britain. There are also a very few Neronian copies, which clearly must be dated after the originals arrived in 64. These official versions seem to have come and gone in an isolated phase; this can perhaps be accounted for by the fact that any attempt to link them to earlier coins would involve Claudian copies, while continuity after 70 would simply involve the ongoing circulation of these coins into the next phase. This does happen to an extent,

17 *Antoninus Pius (138-61) struck several coins depicting Britannia. On this sestertius she is seated on a heap of stones, which may be the wall Antoninus built from (roughly) Glasgow to Edinburgh. She is in warlike pose, with a military standard behind her and a shield with a spike in the centre*

but Neronian bronze is not common in deposits of 100 or 130, as might be expected. This may be due to troop movements – large numbers of Neronian coins brought into the country to pay the army and then moved out fairly soon as the troops were posted elsewhere. Alternatively, it could be a result of coin loss on military sites which subsequently were abandoned. Whatever the answer, this brief influx accounts for the short sharp phase which killed off the Claudian copies.

Possibly there was strict legislation outlawing these coins; but it is more likely that when good new official coin was available the poorly struck, light-weight, old coins simply dropped out of use, and since the latter do not turn up on military sites of the 70s and 80s, this seems to have occurred fairly quickly. In places like Colchester where their production and use flourished, they turn up in layers of the late fourth century and even after the Norman conquest, but this is evidence not of continued circulation, but simply the recycling of disturbed rubbish.

70-260 (?)

The path of Roman coinage in Britain clearly does not run smoothly. First there is a messy period in which the conquest gets lost; then a short period of six years; now comes a length of time in which six generations could be born. The reason is the near-stability of the coinage. Bronze coins of Vespasian (69-79) were still available for hoarding (in a very worn condition) in the 260s,

18 *This as of Antoninus Pius shows Britannia sitting on her heap of stones, but with her head on her hand. Some people see her as sad and brought into line after a revolt, but others see this as wishful thinking*

as the hoards which finish with one or two coins of Postumus (260-8) reveal (**6**). If these collections, which typically contain coins of every ruler from 70 to 200, and then just one or two of 260, were spent instead of being buried and not recovered, those coins of Vespasian would be available for use and loss in the 260s. His silver coins would be rarer, but some still turn up in hoards of the now discontinued denarius in the middle of the third century. As always, the hoard is dated by the latest coin it contains, and so could well be even later than that year.

Once this evidence is taken on board then any attempt to divide the period up is shown to be unrealistic. Equally nonsensical is any attempt to date a site, layer or pit which has one coin of this period in it. The example of the coin of Hadrian, with its still visible and identifiable portrait showing under the clear name and portrait of Postumus, ought to be engraved on every archaeologist's mind. If that coin, worn but recognisable, was available for over-striking in the 260s, it was also available for losing. A worn coin of Hadrian (117-38) in a rubbish pit suggests that the pit was filled in by about 260. This is a matter of probability: the only certain statement that can be made is that the pit cannot have been filled in before the coin was struck. The filling therefore cannot be before 118, may be any time between 118 and 260, but might be 1970 when the coin was disturbed in the digging of a rubbish pit by campers and back-filled with their rubbish, which has since decomposed.

If, on the other hand, the pit contained 20 coins which were without exception of Vespasian, Trajan and Hadrian, then the absence of later examples – which might be expected since they are quite commonly found in Britain

– strongly suggests that the pit was filled by about 150. This illustrates a very important point regarding the use of coins in dating: sometimes, when there is a decent number of coins to judge by, the absence of expected coins is more useful for dating than what is actually there. This 'dating by absence' has raised many archaeological eyebrows in the past; but once it is explained, the eyebrows return to normal. However, in order to make suggestions based on such arguments you have to know both what coins have been struck (for you cannot expect non-existent coins), and even more importantly, what reached Britain. This brings us on to the years after 200.

I mentioned earlier that the occasional hoards of copper coins, whose latest coins belong to the 260s, almost always display a continuous succession of emperors from Vespasian to around 200. This leaves a 60-year gap. Were there no bronze or copper coins struck between 200 and 260? A quick holiday to Italy or the South of France, incorporating a visit to one museum with coins on display, will settle that question instantly; if the display reflects what the museum has in its store-rooms, as opposed to providing an example of a coin by each emperor, then the largest numbers will be bronze coins of 196-260, especially the large bronze sestertii. A trip to a museum in the north of France on the way home will show far fewer of these coins, if any; and back in Britain they are distinctly rare in archaeological contexts. I stress the context because, since they are common in the Mediterranean region, they are common in the coin trade, and therefore there are plenty in Britain; but these arrived in the last three centuries, not 1800 years ago.

So, if our pit with the 20 coins shows examples only from the second century, Hadrian, Antoninus, Marcus Aurelius, and Commodus (180-92), it is wrong to suggest that the pit was probably filled in shortly after 200. It might have been; but we can never know. However, you have to make suggestions on the basis of *expected* coins that are absent, and in Britain any copper coin struck between 200-60 is highly unexpected.

Silver moved a little more quickly because its content changed dramatically from the 180s to the 270s (phases 10-13). As it dropped below 50% in 194 people soon seem to have realised that the old coinage was considerably richer in silver than the new. They acted accordingly, and the older coin was removed from circulation. But for this to happen, the older coins have to be still in circulation, and to pass in front of someone who both is aware of the basic facts, and has some means of benefiting from his knowledge. This accounts for the presence of a few denarii ofVespasian in hoards of silver whose latest coins are of the 250s. All the same arguments apply as to the copper coins, with the extra point to remember being that the old silver coin is a valuable lump of silver, suitable for making into a thin ring, and so worth keeping solely for its metal. Silver plate did not follow the downward slope of the coinage, so far as we know.

This gives us two types of 'residuality', objects turning up in layers where they are far too old for the comfort of archaeologists. We have already seen the worn copper coin, accidentally disturbed by the camper of 1970 digging a rubbish hole, back-filled into the pit with the debris. In this case residuality is due to the recycling of already discarded material. But a silver coin of Vespasian might be kept as a silver good-luck charm, or just as a lump of silver well after other such coins had disappeared from circulation. Once this has happened all forces act to keep it in its 'cared-for' state, because it cannot be fed back into the money market as a coin. When it is eventually lost or deposited it will be far too old for its surroundings, and this has been caused not by discarding but by 'curation'.

So coin-based archaeology in the period 70-260 is the victim of the stability of the Roman coinage. The use of coins was carried along in a fairly unchanging form by the coins sent into Britain, and when this did not occur, the old versions continued to be employed. There are some local reactions to gaps in supply, but we know about them more from the production end rather than the use and loss of the substitute coins produced.

When the denarius was clearly on the way out (phases 10-11), there was a wave of forgery all over the empire, in which Britain participated with enthusiasm. As the new radiate silver coin came in, old denarii were pressed into clay, and moulds were made and fired; these were piled up in columns with runnels between them for the molten metal, and new 'old' denarii were cast. We have these moulds, and we know old denarii were used because the impressions in the moulds are of quite worn coins. But the products are not common as losses on sites in Britain, or anywhere else for that matter. There are a few cast coins and some base coins made from a sort of solder (a mixture of tin and lead which melts at a conveniently low temperature for home coin-making), but this particular phase of forgery never really took off.

I use the word forgery for the first time here in preference to copying, because I think the motive is totally different. Claudian copies were just that, rather rough copies of regular coins which would not have passed a cursory inspection by anyone used to the original. They were also struck in copper, so the gravity of the offence of copying was somewhat uncertain. The denarii cast in the early third century were direct casts from real coins, and therefore looked like real coins: the intent must have been to deceive, and that is my criterion for the charge of forgery. Sometimes the casts used a silver rich metal; on other occasions they did not. Whatever the circumstances this was a far more dangerous undertaking than producing Claudian copies and this may be why the products are far less common.

Recent work in London has unearthed more forgers' moulds, but this time of a far less common variety, which were used partly for the casting of copper coins. True, the real coins very rarely came into Britain, but there seems to have been a good stock of copper coinage already in the province. The effort necessary to produce copper casts seem out of line with the benefits of casting rare sestertii and asses for a fairly well-stocked market. Perhaps this is evidence that the gap in supply was beginning to bite and that, at least in London (the provincial capital), buying, selling and taxation were being affected.

This in turn creates further speculation. We know from the hoards ending with coins of the 260s that there was old currency still about even then. If there really was a need for more coin around the 240s three points emerge. The number of coins in circulation was dropping; this means that they were moving about, being used and lost; therefore the use of coinage in the early third century was either staying level (if the number of new coins produced was equal to the quantity of old ones being lost through natural wastage), or was actually increasing. Remember that this is all speculation based on one fairly recent archaeological find. As with all archaeology, there could be many other explanations which fit the facts equally well; but this set of speculations does raise interesting questions.

260-*c*.330

The collapse of the silver-copper radiate coin to almost zero silver (phases 11-12) seems to have triggered a change in coin supply to Britain. The coppery radiates of emperors such as Gallienus appear in substantial numbers, and are lost with what seems to modern eyes abandon. Few people would trouble themselves to disagree with this simple sentence; but in fact it contains many points which need to be unpacked.

The reign of Gallienus spans two of our earlier periods (phases 12-13), from 253-60 and then 260-8 (we can leave aside the more intricate question of whether it really was 260 as opposed to 259, and accept the former as a notional date). Until 260 Gallienus was second to his father Valerian; afterwards he was on his own, and the legend on the reverses of the coins often give a clue to this. If it shows Pax, peace, as in Pax Augusti (the peace of the emperor) it is shortened to PAX AVG, one G. With two emperors it is Pax Augustorum, shortened to PAX AVGG; three emperors would be AVGGG. An even shorter cut (which is correspondingly even less reliable), is the appearance of the coin. Those of the joint reign usually look silvery; the coins of the single reign look like basic copper. Exceptions abound, but it is a good first clue.

These later coins, struck between 260-8, are now found in Britain in numbers which often equal those of earlier emperors with longer reigns. On many sites, even though there is pottery of the second century, earlier coins simply do not appear, and the total tally of coins of Gallienus may well be more than all the earlier coins combined. So far so good: 'appear in substantial numbers' is clearly acceptable, since if they did not appear in Britain then they cannot be found now.

How about 'lost with what seems to modern eyes like abandon'? Here we reach a thorny issue which for some reason transforms some moderate discussions into heated arguments. We know that these coins are found on Roman sites in Britain today – that is as near a fact as you can get. We know that they appear in layers covered by medieval houses and market places, so they probably reached the deposits in which they were found in the Roman period; again, this is a safe assumption. The matter of dispute is whether they were accidentally dropped and not recovered, or were put on one side as useless and at some time later regarded as rubbish. Were they lost or discarded?

Part of the answer must lie in the place and the time in which they entered the archaeological record. If they got mixed with the mud under a stall on a wet market day when they were still useful current coin, then they were accidentally lost. If they dropped through the floorboards of a cottage as a child was playing with them, years after better coins had been provided by the state, they had been discarded as money and turned into toys. Unfortunately very few sites have been published with enough archaeological detail to decide between these two options. Market stalls leave very little trace, and the dates of deposits usually come from the coins, of which our specimen might be the only example.

Why should anyone discard a coin? The answer almost certainly lies in an old tin or box at the back of a drawer somewhere in your house, which contains farthings or halfpennies, the quarters and halves of old, pre-decimal (1971) pennies, or perhaps the now useless halves of new pennies. Even an old sixpence (now worth 2.5p) or a half crown (12.5p) which looks silvery has little or no value as money. It has been demonetised and it is made of cupro-nickel with not a trace of silver in it, and has neither monetary nor intrinsic value. You may regret the loss of any of these coins by children who are playing shops with them out in the garden for the ever-present reason 'they might one day be valuable', but you will probably not hire a metal detector to find them again. Any of these ideas might be applicable to Roman Britain. The vital point is that the coin can no longer be used simply by going to a shop or market; the ideas apply only when coins have been discontinued in use.

The periods of use and disuse form the guidelines for the phases into which I have divided this commentary. Early Roman silver and copper continues in use in the whole of the western Empire from *c.*75-*c.*260, but after that the only value attached to these coins, so far as we can guess, was the intrinsic value of the metal from which they were made. The current phase runs from 260-*c.*330, and during this period the radiate coins, however base they were, may well have been accepted without question at the market stall. After 330 a few survived, apparently in circulation, but the majority were either removed from or fell out of use. Once they were more or less useless they were probably discarded in increasing numbers. The only way to investigate this is to know the circumstances by which they reached their point of loss.

The drift of the radiate coin from moderate value to very low value has already been described together with the overhaul, or reform, of Aurelian (274) and the Great Reform of Diocletian (294, phase 13-14). British reaction is shaped not only by the nature of the coins and the changes they underwent, but also by supply from the continental mints. The drop from about 5% silver in 260 to around 1% in 270 results in far more of the poorer coins being found today. There were two sources of coin because there were two competing authorities, the Central Empire based in Rome and the Gallic Empire based in Trier and Cologne. The Gallic coin was probably slightly better, taken year by year; both coinages appear in Britain in substantial amounts. The coins of Gallienus (260-8) and Claudius II (268-70) seem to have travelled from Italy without any problem, and those of Postumus (260-8), Victorinus (268-70) and Tetricus (270-3) were presumably supplied from Gallic mints. The poorer coins struck after 268 are more common than the better ones produced before that year. My impression is that the low standard and high supply of coinage in the years around 270 was highly satisfactory for all those who wanted to join in a market economy for the buying and selling of small items of food and household supplies: in fact, things had never been so good.

Then the crash came. Aurelian reformed the coinage (phase 14) and the common coin became 20 times more valuable than it had been: the 5p went and there was nothing lower than the £1 coin with which to buy and sell. The reaction seems to have been very quick. Copies were produced of the earlier radiate coins of very low value, those of Gallienus, Claudius, Victorinus and Tetricus. They all had radiate crowns, they were mostly quite clearly copies, more or less barbarous, so we know them today as Barbarous Radiates (**colour plate 20**). They range from good copies with most of the design and letters following the official pattern closely, through brilliant miniature essays in alternative styles, to ham-fisted blunders in which only the radiate crown can clearly be seen. George Boon once found examples of official coins that were being quartered to produce Barbarous Radiates, so the question of purchasing power is open for discussion: clearly you do not destroy an old coin to produce four new ones unless their total value is greater than that of the coin destroyed.

There is no sign of denominations within the Barbarous Radiates, even though their size varies from *c*.15-*c*.4 mm in diameter. Some show a bit of a silver sheen, and they may well be old radiate coins cut up. Others are clearly of brass rather than copper, the zinc in them makes them paler and more golden, and these may well have come from the old sestertii which disappear at just this time.

Britain is not alone in this rash of copying, for it is well known in northern France, the Low Countries and Germany. Barbarous Radiates do become less frequent as you get further south in France, and there are far fewer in the Mediterranean region. Those that are found there are mostly copies of coins of Claudius II, but these have never been examined in any great detail.

While the production of Barbarous Radiates has been explained as a reaction to the reform of Aurelian and the elimination of official low-value coinage, the issue is probably more complicated. If the new coins were 20 times the value of the old ones, with all other things equal they ought to have entered Britain at the lower rate of one new coin for every 20 old coins that came in; in other words, the actual flow of money into the province ought to have been very roughly constant. But there is a missing link and that is gold.

The main reason for the state to send money to Britain was to pay the state servants, and the most numerous of these were the soldiers and the staff of the governors. In the middle of the third century the choice of pay was either a gold piece a few times a year, or bags of almost worthless silver-copper every week. If board and lodging could be deducted at source from military wages, and requisitioned from the countryside instead of taxes, the need for actual coinage diminished sharply. With your everyday needs met, it was better to have a growing credit in the army accounts settled every so often, or as needed, in gold, than to have to keep a large jar of poor coins of doubtful use hidden in the roof. This all makes perfectly good sense as an idea, but it underlines the problem that gold is usually invisible. It was seldom dropped, nearly always found again, and never discarded because it always maintained its intrinsic value, regardless of the vagaries of the currency system. Archaeologists therefore know little or nothing about it, because it is a very rare sort of find on any excavation. When I say that the archaeological evidence shows a large number of coins entering Britain from 260-74 and a very small number from 274-94, I cannot extend this to say that money supply to Britain followed the same rules. Gold was the greatest element in money supply and, because there is no evidence, we know virtually nothing about its movements at this time.

That said, the new coins struck from 274-94 come into Britain in very small numbers. In fact no; although this might be true, it is not what the evidence actually says. The coins are found today as single finds, in very small numbers. They occur in larger numbers in a few hoards, so they did enter the province, but if they were lost they were searched for, perhaps because of their value.

There are two other possibilities which ought to be aired. There could have been a break in supply of the new silver-copper, and this might be as much a cause of the production of Barbarous Radiates as the high value of these new coins. But we ought to take a quick look outside Britain. In Italy the loss of new radiates is fairly regular: almost as many seem to be lost as of the earlier, poorer coins of Gallienus and Claudius II, although Italy did not indulge in making large numbers of Barbarous Radiates. I have suggested that BRs were needed in Britain to enable people to buy at market stalls. Therefore, Italy either did not have market stalls, or prices there were so much higher that the new coins were completely appropriate to the prices. In either case, Britain seems to be divergent at this time from what evidence we have.

19 *The radiate coinage of Carausius (286-93), struck mainly in Britain, starts out with irregular flans (as here), rather splayed lettering, and quite rough portraiture. The early coins were often without a mint-mark*

20 *However rough his first coins were, Carausius observed the Roman proprieties. Here he is shown arriving formally on the scene in Britain in the approved pose and manner, The Adventus. The mint is London, ML*

21 *In the later part of his reign the image of Carausius and the production of the actual coins sharpened up considerably*

In 286 Britain became even more different from the rest of the empire by forming a separate unit under a rebel emperor named Carausius (**19 & 20**). He had once been in charge of the channel fleet, but was charged with some sort of malpractice. In 286 he retired to Britain, probably keeping a foothold also in northern France, and began to mint his own coins. The first attempts were rather irregular both in shape and lettering, and there were few signs of the 4% silver content then current in coins of the central empire. The portrait was powerful, rough and immediately identifiable. Later issues corrected the earlier crudeness: the flan was well made, the lettering became neat, and the portrait, while still thuggish, was tidied up (**21**).

About 290 Carausius, or the people whom he represented, made three remarkable strokes of propaganda. While the rest of the empire continued with copper-silver, Carausius created a new, fine silver coinage which looked right back to the denarius of the first century (**22 & 23**). To those who knew the old Roman ideals, this was a clear statement of excellence. The state could be judged by the standard of its coinage, and on this level the British state claimed superiority far above the debased central empire. The central emperors, Diocletian and Maximian, only took notice of Carausius to chase and attack him; there was no sign that they regarded him as anything other than a temporary nuisance in the backwoods, who could be eliminated when there was nothing else to do. Yet coins circulated with three portraits, Diocletian in

22 *(left) By the middle of his reign Carausius was producing coins of a high standard. This is a good silver coin with a tidy portrait*

23 *(right) The reverse of* **22** *showing a galley at sea. The legend (FELICITA AVG) records the success of the emperor and below the galley (RSR) is a reference to a line in Virgil's epic meaning 'The Golden Age returns'*

24 *(Obverse): Carausius' blunt diplomacy includes this coin with three emperors, Diocletian in the centre, Maximian nearest us, on his left, in second place, and Carausius in the background in the third place. The legend records (wishfully) CARAVSIVS ET FRATRES SVI, Carausius and his brother emperors. (Reverse): Victory as the COMES AVGGG, the helper of the (three) Augusti, and the mint signature C or G*

the centre, Maximian to the left (the place of honour), and Carausius modestly to the right. The legend proclaimed Carausius and his Brother Emperors (**24**). The brother emperors did not react to coins struck only in Carausius's mints; but then issues appeared of Diocletian and Maximian in the style of their mint at Lyon. The reverses proclaimed the peace of the Augusti, PAX AVGGG – three gs, three emperors (**25 & 26**). To most people it must have looked as if the brother emperors had accepted Carausius's overtures – until they looked at the mint-marks, the Carausian mints of London and C or G, wherever that is.

The final bid for fame came in the form of silver coins with what looked like a mint-mark of RSR under the reverse type (**23**). This was explained in the past as representing coins minted by the Rationalis Rei Summae, the chief of the exchequer. There were also medallions, struck presumably as hand-outs for big occasions, and one had in the exergue the letters I.N.P.C.D.A. Most people despaired of ever decoding this. Then Guy de la Bédoyère was thumbing through his Virgil and came across the line

> Iam Nova Progenies Caelo Demittitur Alto
> Now a new generation is let down from heaven above
> *Eclogues* IV, 6-7

This accompanies a design of Victory in a four-horsed chariot galloping to the right with the legend VICTORIA CARAVSI AUG, the victories of the emperor Carausius. The line above reads Redeunt Saturnia Regna – the

25 *Carausius' needle-sharp diplomacy includes striking coins which look for all the world like ordinary coins of Diocletian, IMP C DIOCLETIANVS PF AVG*

26 *But this, the reverse of* **25** *(in which Diocletian seems to record the PAX AVGGG – the peace due to the (three) Augusti), gives itself away by the mint-mark MLXXI, an XXI coin from the Mint of London*

27 *Around 290 Carausius struck silver coins – something the Central, official, empire did not do. Roman themes predominate, with the wolf and twins and the legend ROMANO R(enewed?)*

kingdoms of Saturn (i.e. the Golden Age) return. RSR occurs on another medallion, as well as some of the fairly normal coinage.

This quite remarkable discovery, which Guy points out should have been made much earlier by for instance eighteenth-century gentlemen reading their Virgil, suddenly brings the British backwoods into the full glare of classical scholarship, which is looking a bit thin even in Rome at this time. It does raise the question of whether Carausius, an up-from-the-ranks sailor, was the driving force behind the monetary policies, the classical allusions, and the military tactics, or whether he was the front thug for a body of people in the north-west of the empire who disliked the way the empire was going enough to band together to try and change it. All Carausius's coinage is Roman in sympathy and statement; it does not represent a breakaway island, but a re-statement of the old ideals of Rome (**27 & 28**). This had been reasonably clear from all the studies which people had done of his coins and their messages, and the Virgilian tags have brought the matter into clearer focus.

Carausius was killed by Allectus in 293, and in 296 the central empire, in the form of the newly promoted Caesar Constantius Chlorus, father of Constantine I, eliminated Allectus in his turn and brought British independence to an end (**29**).

In 294 Diocletian, however resistant he had been to Carausius and Allectus' advances, followed Carausius' lead and re-established a good silver currency (phase 15) (**colour plate 26**). When Britain was regained the empire had just undergone its Great Reform, and the mint in London which had been opened by Carausius was brought into the new Empire-wide system of currency. The

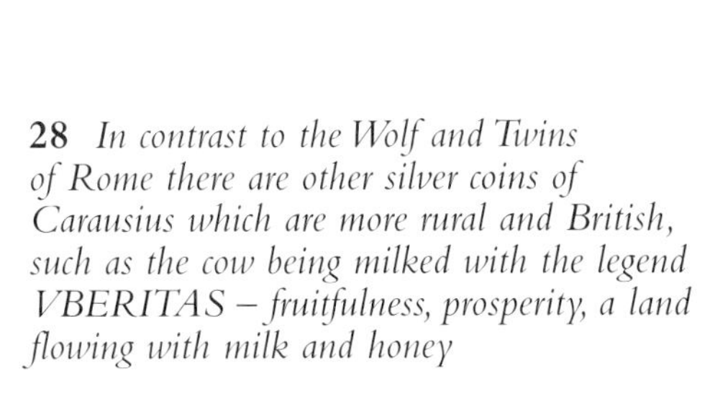

28 *In contrast to the Wolf and Twins of Rome there are other silver coins of Carausius which are more rural and British, such as the cow being milked with the legend VBERITAS – fruitfulness, prosperity, a land flowing with milk and honey*

29 *After Carausius (286-93) came Allectus (293-6). He continued the high standard of portraiture and striking developed in the last years of Carausius*

first official issues from London do not have a mint-mark (**colour plate 27**), which is odd when this was one of the main innovations of the new policy. It has been suggested that this was because Britain, and therefore London, were in disgrace. The mint continued to strike the absolutely normal official coin, with the mint-mark LON or LN, until it closed in about 326; thus Britain produced its own coin from 286-326. Carausius and Allectus had struck gold, good silver, and silver-copper; but the reformed mint struck only silver-copper. This meant that gold and good silver had to brought in from abroad. This period provides a fascinating opportunity to look at the supply of coin to a province, the volumes struck, the times of production and mint closure, the coin which was brought in from abroad, or which simply drifted in through travel and trade – but no one has yet gathered the information, or even taken an interest.

The reformed coinage of Diocletian (phase 15) can be shown from comparison between the coins and Edict on Maximum Prices to cater for all needs, from tanned seal-skin to three pounds of cut grass. This is however only true if all the denominations were struck in decent numbers. There is fairly general agreement that the three silver-copper coins may have values of 25, 5 and 2 denarii: but the smallest coin is extremely rare in archaeology, and not much more common in museums – I have seen only two from Britain, among hundreds of thousands of other coins. They are rare elsewhere as well. In the Mediterranean area the most commonly lost coin of the period is the radiate, 5 denarii; in the north-west it is the 25 denarius piece. Small change was presumably provided by the Barbarous Radiate, but this is a point which needs further thought and attention.

The low value of the BR well equips it to fill the gap between a piece of 25 denarii, a day's wage for a sewer cleaner, and the price of one egg. Britain must have been full of BRs when the reformed mint was established, unless Carausius swept them away. But how can such simple possibilities be tested?

One way forward might be to look at what currency was being hoarded between 290 and 330: but there are several problems. The only date which can be assigned to a hoard is that of the latest coin included. But BRs do not have dates: they are copies, and the only logical dating which can be ascribed is to say that the copy cannot have been produced before the original. If hoards consist of just BRs then they have no hard and fast date. Additionally, a majority of hoards from this period quite sensibly were selective; the person who gathered together a number of official 25 denarius pieces did not normally lower the tone of the collection by throwing in a handful of BRs, and those who did may well not have had access to large numbers of the large coins. Some people who hoarded regular radiates struck up to 274 added a few later coins, but seem to have steered clear of coins of Carausius – this may suggest political choice at work. In the same way there are hoards which are predominantly hoards of Carausius and Allectus. Hoards are chosen for expediency and value, and cannot be used to suggest a cross-section of coin in circulation at the time the collection was buried.

What about coins from excavated deposits? This will one day be the best way of examining the question, but does not work at the moment because so few archaeological reports say what coins were found, and where. Only when we know what coins were found together in what level, and how that level relates to the other deposits on the site, can we judge which levels belong to the period 290-330, and then examine their contents. These will be layers under levels dated by coins of the 320s and 330s, and above those dated by radiates of the 270s. Even when we get this far it will still be difficult to decide whether all the coins found in the layers were in use together, but at least for a quickly built up layer there will be a high probability.

At present I assume that the BRs continued in use to some extent until the next really common coins flooded the market, in 330. Between 294-330 the 25 denarius piece, sometimes called the nummus (or wrongly the follis), either changed completely, or dropped in purchasing power. Both these suggestions are interpretations; what we can actually see is that in this period the most common official coin in circulation got smaller. It may be that if you looked at the numbers of coins found on a site, year by year (and it would have to be a very big or prolific site for that to be possible), and compared the number of coins with their weight you would find a simple link: the numbers would go up as the weight went down, thus keeping the purchasing power lost fairly constant. The difference before and after 330 is partly due to a more sudden change in size and weight in that year, but the picture is clouded by another epidemic of copying.

330-64

This is an action-packed phase which represents the high point of coin use – or at least, coin loss – in Britain. The new coins of 330 (phase 17) must have been about the right value for shopping, because they were used and lost in greater numbers than for any period other than 260-94. The London mint had closed by this time, so coins came into Britain mainly from Trier, now in Germany. Smaller numbers of coins came from Lyon and Arles, now in France.

After some point in 341 the western mints ceased production (phase 17) until somewhere in 345 or 346. It is probably not accidental that most sites in Britain show large numbers of copies of coins from the period 330-41. Some coin experts on the continent find the equation of stoppage of supply and production of home-made copies too slick for comfort, but they are coming round to this way of thinking. It is the same reaction to failure of supply of suitable coin as in the case of the Barbarous Radiate; but whereas most of the latter were clearly barbarous, that is, copies, the Constantinian copies range from the exact to the questionable. Some are the same size as the originals, with virtually perfect lettering, good portraits, and exact mint-marks; it can be just one letter which will give them away, and there are probably other copies so good that they will never be recognised as such. Other copies are very small, yet beautifully engraved and well struck, while some are such loose and imperfect renderings of the original that there is doubt as to what they are copying (**colour plates 30-5**).

This range, which is virtually all struck from engraved dies, means that there is as yet no objective way of telling the good copy from the imperfect original. This in turn means that different people have their own rules for judging copies, and I know perfectly well that my attitudes have changed in the 40 years that I have been identifying coins. When I have a large number of coins in front of me now I separate them into three; a large group which are obviously copies, a smaller selection which are clearly official products, and a medium group which may be one or the other.

As usual, this wave of copying seems to be confined to the north-west provinces, and did not run rampant in the Mediterranean area. This has a knock-on effect, because it automatically means that the high point of coin loss in Britain cannot be directly compared with, for example, Italy; coin loss in this period is lower here, but most of the coins are official products. In comparing the two patterns we may, at this date, simply be saying that the Mediterranean area has few copies.

When the western mints began production again around 345 or 346 they struck at the old standard for two years or so before the reform of 348 (phase 18). The reform produced coins of higher value than before, and as usual the numbers lost, and perhaps used, in Britain declined. After the initial phoenix (representing Rome going into its final century and preparing for rebirth – phase 18), the most common type was that showing a soldier spearing a man who has fallen off his horse – thus known as Fallen Horseman. The official versions of these coins are not common in Britain, but occur in great numbers in the eastern Mediterranean in particular. In Britain, yet another wave of copying occurred, and this time there is never any difficulty (that we know of) in distinguishing between originals and copies. The originals all over the empire are quite large coins, 20mm diameter and over; the copies rarely reach 15mm, and go down to 2 or 3mm. The design goes to pieces, so that very often identification depends on recognising the hindquarters of the horse or the straight line of the spear. These copies often occur in hoards, such as that found at the Roman temple at Lydney on the west bank of the river Severn (**colour plates 36-7**).

A warning needs to be inserted here because of the ideas which circulated as a result of this find. The newspapers of the time went to town on 'King Arthur's Small Change', and the date of the hoard was pushed far into the fifth or sixth century. Fallen Horseman types were not the only copies that were given dates well into the post-Roman period; it happened to the Barbarous Radiates as well. At one stage serious academic papers were written to suggest that the Saxons who invaded Britain in the fifth century particularly went for copies of the Radiates, while the hard-pressed Britons preferred the Fallen Horsemen. We now know that the Lydney 'date' was the result of an archaeological mistake which was influenced by widespread wishful thinking. This error has been corrected by the more recent work of John Casey.

Barbarous radiates have been put back into the period 270-330, and Fallen Horseman copies confined to 350-70, but people still hanker for a fifth-century

30 *(left) This silver coin of Constantius II has been clipped, with the outer rim removed but the legend left. You can even see where the clipping started and finished – they do not quite meet*

31 *(right) The coin of Julian (355-63) is complete, and shows what has been lost in the clipping of* **30**

coinage, and there are outbreaks of wishful thinking every so often. The fifth century will be dealt with later, but the copies belong here. The main point at issue is that when examples of all the different groups of copies can be firmly anchored in dated deposits, there is nothing left which needs to be assigned a floating date in the post-Roman period. There is no type of either Barbarous Radiate or Fallen Horseman which is known only in post-Roman contexts. This means that if people want to give late dates to some of these coins, they can only do so to a random sample of what was already made, used and lost in an earlier period when the originals were still about.

The copies of 335-45 and 350-60 all seem to be swept away with the substantial issues of the House of Valentinian starting after 364. Meanwhile silver left the silver-copper coins, so that by the start of the next phase state production of low-value coinage was in copper.

364-402

The way these sections are divided implies that coin usage changed dramatically at given dates. This is clearly not true; there was instead a gradual shift, which was less gradual at some times than at others. So the year 364 saw the beginning of a new dynasty, a new system of copper coinage – but to the man

32 *This gold solidus is of the emperor Magnus Maximus (383-8). He started his imperial career in Britain, and may have struck the gold in the London Treasury into coin to pay his soldiers before they set out for the mainland of Europe to install him as full emperor. Victory hovers over the two emperors. Below them AVGOB suggests a coin minted in OB(ryzium), refined gold, at AVG(usta), a name by which London was sometimes known in the later empire*

or woman at the market stall, the mixture was very much as before. The new coins came in to Britain in quite large numbers, were hoarded, used and lost. When they were hoarded they were sometimes kept quite separate from what had gone before, but the smaller hoards (which may well have been just the contents of a purse) show a mixture of coins, with issues going way back to scruffy radiates.

Since these coins were not commonly copied it is possible to compare coin loss in Britain with elsewhere. Britain and the Danube frontier show high levels; the Mediterranean area maintains its usual pattern, with a small number of coins lost regularly each year. This might suggest that the high loss in Britain of coins of 330-48 is a real feature rather than just the product of copying; but more work is needed.

There is one point at which Britain and the Danube connect, and this is seen in an unusual mint-mark. The contribution of Trier to coin supply for Britain drops sharply after military troubles on the Rhine around 350-5, and there is a corresponding rise in issues from Lyon and Arles. Then suddenly, in around 370, just one of the many marks used by the mint of Siscia (modern Sisak) appears in Britain. If there are ten coins of the House of Valentinian from a site it is quite likely that one of them will have the usual SISC below the reverse type, but then either side of the figure of the emperor, or victory, there will be the letters R over A with a loop on top and F (**colour plate 40**). This is usually the only Siscia mint-mark to occur in any numbers in Britain, but it is not common at home in the Balkans, and I have not tracked it down elsewhere. This has been commented on many times, and there are two preferred explanations: either the mint at Siscia bagged up one issue and sent most of them to Britain, or soldiers who had just been paid in the Balkans were transferred to Britain with full purses.

A detailed study might be able to decide between these two possibilities. If the coins were bagged up at the mint and sent to Britain, then they would probably have been struck from a small number of dies in a short time. This would mean that if the coins in Britain were photographed, and the results collected and compared, many would be absolutely identical because they were struck from the same dies. If however they had been sent out into normal circulation in the Balkans and the soldiers had simply brought a random sample over to Britain, the coins would be far more varied, and what we call die-linking would be almost invisible. The study has not yet been done – the coins are out there, ready and waiting. I give this detail as an example of the many aspects of the study of coinage in Britain which a reliable and hard-working person could start on with very little preparation. Reliable because museums who guard the coins need to know who they are dealing with; hard-working because the coins are scattered all over Britain, and there will be no nice juicy results until a fair number of close-up photographs have been taken. This is not a project which would lead to instant gratification, but it is one which would deserve to get the person's name in print.

Coins of the House of Valentinian are periodically misused to connect sites to a non-event called the Barbarian Conspiracy, which one ancient source gives as occurring in 367. I am being naughty in calling something which is well described in a decent Roman source a non-event, but I do it because so many people swallow what the sources say with uncritical abandon. There was trouble, a high-ranking officer was sent to deal with it, and lives were lost. The problem is that once this 'event' gets into the textbooks anyone who discovers a coin of the house of Valentinian among the ashes of a burned-down hut immediately invokes the Barbarian Conspiracy – and these are the well-behaved archaeologists. There are plenty of others who will jump on the band-wagon with no more evidence than that their hut burned down sometime after 348. Such use of the coins of the house of Valentinian is pushing the evidence very hard. The coin has to be struck in Lyon or Arles late in 364 at the earliest. It then has to be sent out and put into general circulation. The occupants of a farmstead who only go to market once a month have to get this particular coin in change from a market trader with no hot links to the Roman treasury, take it home, and lose it before the Barbarians descend to burn his hut. Such a chain of events is not impossible, but the majority of such coins must have been lost after, rather than before 370.

After the rush of coins of 364-78 there is a lull. The coins are produced in the mints and are lost in other provinces, but few are lost in Britain between 378-88. This gap in supply does not result in immediate copying.

After 388 coin came into Britain in quite large amounts, but it is more common in some areas than others. In a very detailed study Nick Ryan found a particular concentration of such coins in the Cotswold/Oxford region, and the Roman fort at Richborough produced over 20,000 examples. Silver coins are sometimes found, and even gold may turn up occasionally.

The fact that silver coins are found to constitute about one coin in a thousand on any site in Britain occupied at the time is worth a comment. This is higher than on sites almost anywhere else in the Empire, but no clear explanation has yet been suggested. We can eliminate discard as the reason, because however dim a view people who study the history of Rome take of Little Britons, the throwing away of lumps of silver is unlikely. Britain does have several sources of the metal in the Mendip Hills, the Peak District and Flintshire, so the number of silver coins may in some way be related to the mineral resources. In the same way Britain shows an abnormally high occurrence of buried and unrecovered hoards of silver plate of the late fourth century; and there may be a connection here. A difference needs to be noted between hoards of silver coins or silver plate, and the casual loss and non-recovery of individual silver coins, which is probably accidental and needs no extra explanation. Burial of precious things is not necessarily a standard thing to do – it varies in the Roman empire both in time and in region. The third century in Gaul saw the burial of a lot of silver; but in the Balkans, where the troubles were at least as pressing, the practice apparently did not occur. Burial of plate in Britain in the period 380-450 is common, whereas in Gaul it is almost unknown.

The last copper coins seem to have entered Britain by about 402; silver arrived in very small amounts from 408-11, and then virtually stopped. The gold record is always poor, but hoards die away in the early part of the fifth century.

The strange thing here is that although there is a clear halt in supply of copper after 402, and Britain had an excellent record for copying coins when new batches were not supplied, there are no copies in the early fifth century. I can state this because some of all the copies we recognise are found close to their originals in the layers of all sites, and there are no other copies to fit into this gap. The reason is quite simple – there was no point. Copper was intrinsically worthless unless a state promised to exchange it for gold or silver, and this could only work when the state supplied gold and silver coins. After 402 there was no ruling state to supply gold and silver coins and there were certainly no promises to exchange copper scraps for valuable metal, so there was no point in striking funny designs on little scraps of copper.

When is post-Roman? The fifth century

Any investigation of the British reaction to Roman coinage after 402 has to take into account two things: the facts and the fantasies. The facts are thin on the ground; the fantasies grow like weeds. My problem is that I am content to stick to the facts, admit that there is little to know and agree that we know only little of that. To some people that is defeatist – we can know more; to others it is pointless, because what they want is a story which satisfies how they want the past to have been.

That version is based on the present, and this is where the trouble sets in. It is quite clear that since I cannot do without coinage the people of the fifth century would have felt the same way. So coinage must be created for them – or rather, coinage must be created to satisfy what I see as their wants. The people of the year 399 used coinage; some of them lived until 450; they would clearly have continued to use it. People do not just give things up without a struggle you know. Roman coins are found in Saxon huts and cottages, so they were used and lost in those places. Since they were used and lost in Saxon Britain, just as in Roman Britain, the use of Roman coins continues from the late fourth century until the Saxon coinage was fully established. Life went on; trade went on; and you cannot have life and trade without coins.

My reaction to these arguments is one of deep depression. It might be much simpler just to finish this section with a bland statement such as: after 400 we move into the Early Middle Ages and that is another world, another story. But a teacher has a basic tendency to try to teach, however patronising that sounds, and if I can see major faults in the lines set out above I regard it as a total failure of nerve if I do not try to explain why things have gone adrift.

We can start with silver and gold, and there may be a measure of agreement between fact and fantasy here. Coined silver gets progressively rarer in the fifth century throughout the surviving empire, or the dismembered empire. The substantial number of silver coins of the years 357-411 known in Britain is divided into three main forms: perfect, with the outer rim cut off, and finally with the lettering clipped off, leaving only the portrait intact. With the outer rim gone the coin is lighter in weight, but all the communication is there. With the letters clipped the individuality has gone, but the imperial image is intact. In a sense the Britons are taking one stage further the late Roman tendency to ignore the individual and concentrate on the imperial status – and gaining a nice bag of clippings into the bargain. It could well be that an injured emperor – a gash across the face, or a clip into the head – is evidence of a thought crime which is punishable by death. An attack on the imperial image is, in a legal sense, an attack on the emperor. When the image is on silver or gold which is somehow as sacra (sacred) and set apart as the emperor himself, and only on loan to the user, the crime is increased. It would be better to melt down a coin with a wounded image along with the clippings.

When did this clipping happen? At present we do not know, but the general feeling is that the process of supply had only recently ended, and clipping starts as supply runs down. Even clipped coins are not always very worn, so they have probably not seen much hand-to-hand circulation. However they might have gone on in clipped form in sets of 100 coins or so in a bag for decades after the last new coin appeared in Britain. It might seem that this is a move towards fantasy, but if so it is one with which I am happy, because the exchange of bags of silver has moved away from the use of coin. The silver has its own value regardless of the shape or form of the piece, and totally removed from the messages stamped on it. At one time the messages acted as guarantee of the standard, but there is probably enough left on them to be reasonably sure that they are of a good silver content. If these bags of silver coin did change hands in the later fifth century, then they never entered the archaeological record when the bags were emptied and the silver was used for making something else. They were also never buried on post-Roman sites, whether Saxon or British. But if you want to believe in the continued used of lumps of silver throughout the fifth century I will not try to convince you otherwise, so long as you do not call the process 'coin-use'.

Gold provides less evidence, but at present what does exist is fairly clear. A recent find is the Patching hoard of gold coins of the fifth century, which must have been buried towards the end of the century in Sussex. Coins of the sixth and seventh century have been found, in some cases mounted in Anglo-Saxon jewellery. One quarter of a gold tremis (a third of a gold piece), with signs of craft-working, was found in a deposit in Canterbury. I accept without reservation that gold coins entered Britain in small numbers from 400 until about 700, but I think the vital point is that these were pieces of gold – the jewellery and the cut tremis – as opposed to negotiable coins.

With copper coins in post-Roman contexts the picture is reasonably clear. First we can reject the idea that the coins of *c.*400 went on in circulation into the sixth century. In the first place the majority of Roman sites that have been excavated simply do not show layers above those which are full of fresh late Roman coins and freshly broken late Roman pottery. These layers tend to come at the top of a sequence in which coins supply a general sequence of dates, and the latest levels are probably of the years around 400. Most Roman sites then stop – they do not run down, the layers do not get thinner and peter out, there is not massive evidence of fire or destruction, they just stop. Where stratigraphy does continue, for example in Saxon Winchester, the coins in the later layers form a complete sample of all the coins which ever circulated on the site, from the first century to the fourth, and they are not the same in composition as the layers of the late fourth century. This tells me that the coins in the later layers which show no recognisable pattern of change from one type to another are the result of recycling rubbish: the digging of rubbish pits and foundations, graves and post-holes.

The earth from such activities contains a sample of earlier coinage, and this gets incorporated in Saxon layers. If you want to believe in the continued use of fourth century coinage into the fifth and sixth century, then you must provide me with deposits which show similar groups of coins to those that were lost in the late fourth century in layers higher up the stratigraphy. At present these do not exist, so I will continue to combat what I see as your faulty belief.

Ah! but there are Saxon sites with no Roman counterparts underneath, where Roman coins still turn up. So when people left the Roman sites they took their coinage with them to the new Saxon locations. No, that will not work either; the lists that have been made of such finds show a run of issues over the whole spread of Roman coinage, often with an interest in earlier heavy bronze sestertii which were useful for metal or as weights. This does not show continuity, because the coins in question do not represent the last lot of issues that were in Roman use. They have been gathered by exactly the same process as they are today, by walking over Roman sites which are being ploughed or worked. Saxon Roman coins in bulk are very like the produce of an afternoon's metal detecting on a good site. So yes, the Saxons do seem to have been interested in Roman coins, to have collected them, used them as weights, put them in burials, made necklaces of them, and perhaps even used them as tokens in exchange – but this process is separate from the last days of coin use in the fourth century because the coins themselves are different. Now that we have a good sample of coins from Saxon sites we can say that they were not particularly interested in very barbarous Radiates or scruffy Fallen Horsemen; they had higher standards.

This leaves us with a gap in coin use in fifth-century Britain. I think the explanation for this relates to the matter of intrinsic versus token value. Gold and silver, whether coined or not, have their own worth. Whole, or clipped, or cut precious metal coins may well have changed hands in the fifth century just as gold dust did in ancient Egypt. The use of copper coins is a completely different matter; these do not carry their own value, they have an imaginary value set on them by an organisation which persuades you to believe in it. The moment either the organisation or the belief fails, the value is lost. When there was a gold and silver coinage the simplest way to get people to believe in copper was to allow them to use it in buying 'real' value in bullion. If you can collect 7200 nummi, the gold piece is the prize (phase 21), and even if you never see more than 100 nummi in a month, the possibility is still there. Should the state starts to change things or, even worse, the supply of gold dries up, your copper is just so much scrap metal.

Have you still got that half-crown? It has a metal value, but it is very low. Why do you not sell it for its metal? Because it is still worth something – even if only half a crown: and the alternative of 12.5p is ridiculous, because a half-crown was worth far more than that. But in fact it is not worth anything in that sense because the system has moved on and left all the pre-decimal coins to their fate – the coin dealer or the children's playbox. In just the same way the system moved on from token coinage early in the fifth century, and the idea that small lumps of copper had a make-believe value went out of fashion.

The Anglo-Saxon coinage, which starts off in gold in the mid-600s, does belong to the early Middle Ages, and it really is a different story. Copper coinage with a token value is something that is not seen again in Britain for 1000 years.

3 Hoards

General ideas on hoards

A coin hoard from the Roman period consists of money that was buried or set aside, and has now been found. If it was not set aside it is not there to find – if it has not been found we know nothing about it. It consists of coins which may vary from the high value of one gold piece all the way down to a few scruffy bronze coins (**colour plates 23-4**).

There are two ways of looking at hoards of coins in Roman Britain, or anywhere else for that matter, and they can be summed up as with excitement or depression. In the first case there is expectation, and the certainty that here is something out of the ordinary! This is the exclamation made by people who look at a hoard in admiration for a few minutes and then go on to the next sensation. The second way evokes more of a groan: here is yet another group of coins which demand a large amount of hard and not very exciting work in order to make a record of them, and here is another chance for fantasies to be weaved and wrong-headed prejudices to be given yet another airing. This is the exclamation often made by people whose job it is to examine and record hoards. Hoards of coins can thus open up the divide between the coin worker and the public so that each side goes away even more convinced of the folly of the other.

One major disagreement comes from the idea of what is interesting. It seems reasonable to say that if those coin people make a fuss about one copper coin, then a hoard of silver coins must be more interesting – but this confuses intrinsic value with valuable information. The kilogram of silver in the hoard has a quite definite market worth, and the fact that it is in the form of coins adds to this. But the fact that the coins are all nearly 2000 years old does not necessarily create yet further added value: a kilo of Roman coins, of which many other thousands of similar examples exist, is less valuable on the market than 50g of rare medieval silver coins. It is a matter of supply and demand – if there are plenty, the price is lower; if they are rare the price is higher, provided a lot of people want them. When the coins from a hoard have been shared out, or sold in lots, then they are exactly the same as other coins of their type. 'But I paid a lot for these, they came from the famous hoard.' Well, of course I believe you, but how are you going to convince the person to whom you hope to sell them (especially as he can buy exactly the same thing for half the price elsewhere)?

33 *A sestertius of Antoninus Pius (138-61), with a nearly perfect portrait and excellent lettering emphasising that ANTONINVS was first AVG(ustus), and then given the title PIVS. He was PP, father of the country, and, as always, TRP, holder of the Tribunician Power*

That is one problem with coins from hoards: in the majority of cases they are exactly the same, one by one, as those not from hoards. This makes sense because the year before the hoard was buried and never recovered, all sorts of coins were circulating together and no one knew which coins would just be lost in the market place and which would be gathered together to hide under the apple tree.

There is of course a second problem with coin hoards and the market. Coins gathered together to bury tend to be issues in circulation together at the same time. So in the reign of Hadrian (117-38) there will a large number of coins of the last emperor Trajan (98-117) to chose from. There is a market price today for an ordinary, common, denarius of Trajan, but that may be dented when a hoard of 2000 similar coins suddenly comes on the market. If nothing else, coins found in hoards are generally in better condition than those found singly, because their lives in circulation have been cut short by burial. A hoard therefore tends to flood the market with good examples, and medium or poor examples may become hard to sell.

After the hard work has been done and the hoard recorded and published, the problems which produce the groans relate not so much to the coins themselves but to the ideas which spin, and get spun, around them. A hoard of silver coins, the last of which is dated to *c.*AD 50, is clearly yet another example of the disaster which hit so many people during the revolt fixed to the name of Boudica – otherwise Queen Boadicea – in the years 60 or 61. Hoards buried about 270 are evidently the result of Major Trouble, clearly related to the Barbarian Invasions on the mainland of Europe. Hoards buried around 400 just demonstrate where the invading Saxons did their worst. In fact to many people hoards equal hordes – ravening or raving, pillaging and looting and, in other words, fun, or at least rather more interesting than the usual dull stories that historians and archaeologists trot out. If that is what you want to believe, then no one can take it away from you; yet you are missing so much. It probably does not matter that your house of interpretation is built upon sand, because if the foundations are undermined by proper research you will simply shift your castle into the air where it is safe from all attack.

What do hoards mean?

Let us nibble at the problems bit by bit. You say that hoards of 270 clearly show Barbarian Invasions in Britain, and you got the idea from historical sources which talk about major invasions in Germany and Gaul. What about hoards of 120? No, there are no records of invasions anywhere in Europe around this time – so what do those hoards represent? But perhaps there are no hoards deposited around 120. Before we can argue about the meaning of hoards at a given date we need to know how that date compares with others. If the number of hoards in 270 (the time of the German Invasions) is less than the number in 120, then the connection is clearly very weak. I would add that we also need to know how hoarding varies round the empire. It would be faulty to pick on a peak in Britain in 270 and conclude that hoards equal hordes, if there was a similar concentration in North Africa, where we are fairly sure all was peace and prosperity.

Up to about AD 2000 these simple points could not have been settled because the study which would give the basic facts simply had not been done, or published. Now we have the great work of Prof. Anne S. Robertson (ASR) in print, and that of Peter Guest (PG) is on its way to publication. ASR has made available a list of coin hoards found in Roman Britain which totals about 1500; PG has surveyed the western Roman Empire less intensively, but it gives a basis on which to start work. A summary of the hoards listed by ASR is shown in Table I.

The hoards are put in chronological periods which usually correspond those in which the production of Roman coinage was described. In some cases however the periods are longer – 317-48, instead of 317-30 and 330-48. This is because so many hoards were recorded in what today is incomplete form. Thus to say a hoard ends with coins of Constantine can give any date between the accession of Constantine I in 306 and the death of Constantine II in 340. To mention Constantius is even worse: Constantius I became emperor in 293 and Constantius II died in 361.

The total is the number of hoards mentioned by ASR, but this is broken down in several ways. 'Good' and 'Bad' are shorthand for the information that is available in the ASR volume. 'Good' in the early periods usually means that the emperors are listed with the number of coins attributed to them – as Trajan 56, Hadrian 72. 'Bad' means information that states 'a hoard was discovered among which were coins of Hadrian'. Not only were we not told whether the coins were silver of bronze, but we know neither all the emperors nor the number of coins for each. Generally, up until 294 and the Great Reform of Diocletian, 'good' hoards provide enough information for future work, while 'bad' instances are simply hoards of likely dates in known places, on which work can go no further.

Table I Coin hoards in categories

Date	Total	Good	Bad	Gold	Mix	Silver	Mix	Bronze	Uncertain
To 41	18	15	3	1	1	13	-	1	2
41-54	26	10	16	5	2	4	2	11	2
54-69	11	7	4	1	1	5	-	3	1
69-96	60	38	22	7	5	17	8	13	10
96-117	21	12	9	-	-	11	3	3	4
117-38	43	21	22	1	2	20	7	7	6
138-61	66	44	22	1	3	29	9	9	15
161-80	97	62	35	-	1	62	10	20	4
180-92	35	17	18	-	2	16	1	8	8
193-222	49	22	27	-	-	31	4	7	7
222-38	31	22	9	-	-	26	1	2	2
238-60	36	13	23	-	-	28	1	2	5
260-96	530	287	243	-	-	515	2	12	-
296-317	99	-	99	-	-	-	-	99	-
317-48	195	-	195	2	-	-	-	193	-
348-64	119	-	119	1	-	2	2	114	-
364-411	280	-	280	12	14	59	13	182	-

After 294 I am sorry to say that all hoards are listed as 'bad', because whatever information was contained in the original publication has been given in the book by emperor. Unfortunately this means that further work based on the book is impossible, and anyone who wants proper information must go back to the original publication. The other categories are gold, gold and silver

mixed, silver, silver and bronze mixed, bronze and uncertain. The lesson here is that if you want to run gold through your fingers you have to find a hoard of the last fifty years of the empire in Britain, for these are more numerous than gold hoards of any other date.

If we go by crude numbers then I am already clearly under siege. We told you so: 260-90, 530 hoards, more than in any other period, clearly indicating trouble. There are both ways in which the numbers can be evened out, and features of this period which do not occur at any other time, but in general it is true to say that this is a time of intensive hoarding. Or is it?

A major problem emerges here: information on coin hoards is one of the oddest sets of information left from the ancient world. While all evidence is biased to some extent, coin hoards are probably the only type which is totally so. The reason is quite simple. Many coins were gathered together at different times, put in a pot, a box, or a leather bag, and buried in the field, stuffed into the roof, or put behind the round stone loose in the wall. A number of these hoards, almost certainly the majority, were recovered, taken back to market and exchanged for a cow and a calf. These we not only do not, but cannot, know anything about. The only coin hoards that we know about are those which failed – for some reason, no one went back to recover them. We therefore *must not* talk about times of intensive hoarding, but we can talk about times of intensive non-recovery.

There is one more negative point before we can return to being positive. Talk about hiding and non-recovery leaves out of account those groups of coins that were deposited, rather than hidden, with no intent to recover them. To give a modern example: when you want flowers to take to your old aunt in hospital you do not go out to the nearest cemetery where there has just been a funeral and lift the flowers from the heaps on the latest grave. I use this example which a few people may consider in bad taste exactly for that reason; there is not only the matter of honesty, but there is the extra point of the strong disapproval of the people around you. So the person who put a small purse-full of coins in the pool dedicated to the nymph could be reasonably sure that social pressure would leave it there until it was covered over by dead leaves and pond weed. Certainly the goddess Coventina who was worshipped near the fort at Carrawburgh on Hadrian's Wall kept away from her well any who hoped for a quick dip into the monetary offerings, with the result that in the nineteenth century (when her strength had waned) at least 16,000 coins were dug out.

Coventina's Well in fact appears in ASR's book, but with a cautionary note. There is absolutely no question that large numbers of coins were found in the well in the nineteenth century, but the problem in interpretation is twofold. Since they span most of the Roman period in Britain, with a heavy concentration in the first 250 years, it seems likely that they were not all thrown in at one time, but singly over decades, or in small groups. If the 16,000 are spread over a mere 200 years that only gives 80 coins a year. If we invent a

Good Luck ceremony on 1 May, it only needs 60 men from the nearby fort to invest one copper coin for good luck to make up a high proportion of the annual total. On this sort of interpretation, this collection is nothing like the usual hoard, in which coins are gathered together and buried at one moment in time. But Bruce MacKay, who listed the coins, thought that he could see a clump, perhaps of the later second century, within the general run, and he therefore suggested the possibility of a bag of coins being thrown down the well in addition to the yearly offerings. This is the point which has gained the doubtful note from ASR. Since it must be a matter of speculation based on numbers, and we do not yet know much about the general run of numbers in copper hoards in Britain, and anyway the annual offerings would get badly in the way of the numerical analysis of any possible hoard, we have to leave the question open. I think MacKay was quite right to raise the possibility, and equally that it was reasonable of ASR to question it.

So Coventina's Well warns us of the likelihood that there are at least two variations on the theme of 'lots of coins deposited in antiquity', which could be called instant deposits and continual offerings. Unfortunately, it is traditional in coin studies to imagine other types of deposits – savings, emergency, and so on. This is not so much wrong, as absolutely pointless. Instant deposits can usually be distinguished from continual offerings by inspection of their composition. Coventina's Well is an excellent case in point; the latest coins from the find belong to the second half of the fourth century, but the bulk of the issues are of the second century. Our present understanding of the coinage available for hoarding in the later fourth century is totally against such a composition. There is absolutely no evidence that anyone in the fourth century had access to such large numbers of coins, over 150 years old, from general circulation. Of course one fourth-century hoarder could have raided Coventina's Well and totally confused us by burying the loot with a few choice fourth-century coins elsewhere. That, as an instant deposit, would have a unique composition among others of this variation. It would also have been a remarkably stupid instant deposit, because its value lay completely in the few current coins and the scrap value of the old bronze coins from the well.

Different types of hoard

But why am I so dismissive of the idea of savings hoards, purse hoards and emergency hoards? I do not so much reject the ideas as their application. No one who has talked about such hoards has provided any methods of identifying the one from the other, and no studies on the analysis of hoards has shown any major distinguishable groupings within their composition. Hoards of denarii ending with Commodus (180-92) have a generally similar composition, within which there is a continuum of change. In other words, there are some hoards with more coins before Hadrian (117-38), some with more from 150-80, and a majority of hoards which fill in between the two extremes in a smooth progression. All this lies within an overall composition which is different from that of hoards ending with Hadrian or Septimius Severus (193 to 211). If different groups of hoards cannot be distinguished by fairly careful numerical study, and the people who fantasise about different categories of hoards cannot tell us how they may be different when found, then what is the point of the discussion?

The point, I will be told, is that we must think about the reasons behind the hoarding. This is material evidence from the ancient world and it must be made to tell us something in human terms. Numbers of coins of each emperor, or even worse, percentages, tables and diagrams get us nowhere in human terms – they are simply a more complicated statement of the obvious facts. This view provides lots of points for dissection.

In the first place, as I pointed out above, we can never know anything about hoarding in general because it is a fair guess that the majority of hoards were totally successful and we can therefore never know anything about them. We can either discuss unrecovered hoards, and stick to reality, or fantasise about all the hoards that were ever buried. As much as I enjoy reading fantasy, I like to be able to separate it from fact. In this case writing about hoarding is always fantasy; discussion of unrecovered coin hoards may, in some cases, be fact.

The second point is a very general one. I accept completely the charge that to pull hoards to pieces and put their compositions in diagrams of percentages is to state the obvious. The reason for doing it is to underline similarities and differences between hoards, and to state the obvious in a more intelligible way. But the moment you cease to state the obvious you move into fantasy. This is a good thing to do, provided you know that you are doing it, and your audience knows this as well. The moment you move from a statement of what was in a hoard, or how this hoard compares with that hoard, to why this hoard is here, you move from something which can be done on simple logical lines to an area of discussion where logic cannot form the basis for progress.

Let us take a special hoard such as that from Falkirk in Scotland. Its last coin is of Severus Alexander (222-35), but its composition, judged by numbers of coins of different emperors, is totally different from other hoards which end with his coins. Judged qualitatively there is no coin in that hoard which does not occur in the other hoards of similar date. The type of coin in our hoard is normal for the date; the distribution through time is not. Aha! an odd hoard – perhaps evidence for emergency or savings or a purse. Wait a moment. Take away the coins after 222 and look at it again. The numbers now are indistinguishable from most of the hoards of coins whose latest coin is of Septimius Severus and his family (193 to 222). So far the steps have been totally mathematical and logical. I think – note this phrase – I think that the simplest explanation for the strange composition of this hoard is that it was formed during the years 193–222, kept, perhaps buried and dug up again, who knows, and then in the period 222–35 a few 'new' coins were added and the whole collection was buried. The new coins may have been of any date, not just of the current emperor, so the whole composition of the hoard may have changed a little. The only point at which this shows in the numbers is for coins after 222.

The moment interpretation came in we moved from fact to fantasy: from stating the obvious to saying something interesting. There are several other possible explanations – in fact if likelihood is disregarded there is an almost infinite number. Perhaps the hoarder disliked the current regime and got hold of as many 'old' coins as he could; in a momentary panic he added the contents of his purse and buried the lot. Maybe the hoarder had heard that old coins were of better silver, so it made better sense to collect those. This was true, in a way, but the cut-off date for better silver was 194 when the denarii were debased, so the hoarder was a bit out. Neither of these special pleadings can be proved wrong, and neither can be proved right. But the discussion of numbers is either consonant with the known information on coin hoards (right), or it is not (likely to be wrong). This is what I mean by fact and fantasy.

What the hoards say

Through all this I seem to be ignoring the information held in the hoard itself which should tell us why it was deposited and not recovered. Many people reading that seemingly sensible sentence will see the problem, but I will spell it out. The soldier who buried a small hoard of denarii in the field did it because he did not trust the other people who slept in the surrounding bunks. He did not know when he hid it that when he returned to the barrack block a friend would give him a message that he was to report immediately to the commander, and insist on taking him directly there himself. There was nothing particularly to worry about because his conscience was clear. But he was such a good chap that the commander insisted that only he could escort the distinguished visitor, just about to depart, to the next fort; and so it goes on. He did in fact write to a friend to tell him about the hoard, but he had it all in his mind's eye, and one hawthorn bush is very much like another unless you know where you buried your money.

That is a slightly longwinded way of saying that a hoard which was buried with intention to recover it, but was found today (and was clearly therefore not recovered), by its very nature cannot carry inside it the reasons for non-recovery. If our soldier had known the events even one hour ahead he would not have buried his hoard. Non-recovery of all but votive deposits is accidental.

34 *A sestertius of Commodus (180-92) only thirty years later than* **33** *but showing the typical shape of the years around 200, with straight edges and corners. He sets out his full titles including PM (Pontifex Maximus – chief priest): TRP XIIII – holder of the Tribunician Power for the fourteenth time, IMPVIII – hailed as Imperator for the eighth time, COS V – consul for the fifth time, and finally PP – Pater Patriae, father of the country*

There you are, proved it. Hoards equal hordes. Pillage and plunder. Well, yes: and promotion, genuine mistakes, forgetfulness, and accidental intrusion by others. So how do you sort out pillaging and plunder from the rest? It is obvious: none of the things like promotion or forgetfulness come in epidemics – invasions do. We are back once again to numbers. Gentle backgrounds of forgetfulness and promotion give a gentle continuum of non-recovery. Peaks of trouble will be seen in peaks of non-recovery.

Then is there nothing in the coins themselves which might help interpretation? Modern parallels are always dangerous because there is no way of knowing whether ideas can be back-dated. 'It is obvious – people are just like that' is one of the first faulty ideas that has to be knocked out of any first-year archaeology student's head. One extreme way to do it would be to transplant each student to a background radically different from their own for six months. They would come home quite sure that though many aspects of human action are similar, there is no sure agreed basis on which interpretations can be built. But if I go to my cupboard one of the first things I will find is that battered folded envelope containing about thirty farthings. These quarters of the old, pre-decimal, penny went out of use in the 1940s, before the great decimal change of 1971. In theory four of them would have made a penny right up to 1971, but they were in limbo for 20 years. a theoretical part of a monetary system but one that was not in practical use. As they went out of use I collected them, not in a collector's sense but by seeing them come in and not letting them go out again. When decimalisation came in they had been useless for a long time, but at that point they ceased to be part of the current system. I still have them, kept safely, hoarded in a sense, and I have no intention either of offering them to a coin dealer or throwing them away. They might come in useful.

This is one of the possibilities that has to be faced when the bulge of hoards from the period 260-94 is examined carefully. It is also a reason why a general knowledge of the production of Roman coinage, and the participation of Britain in the general system, is essential before getting down to details of interpretation. A recap is needed.

The coinage system gradually changed through the third century from the balance of bronze and denarii of 50% silver in 200, to an absence of bronze and a single radiate coin (perhaps a relic of the old double denarius) with 1% silver on good days around 270. Bronze seems to have dropped out of circulation, and some of it seems to have been used to make Barbarous Radiates. Good silver was clearly at a premium, and both layers of site-finds and the contents of hoards strongly suggest that silver of even 50% fineness had disappeared soon after 270. In 273 there were 1% silver radiates, and apart from variable gold, that was it. Then Aurelian reformed the coinage; he stabilised the gold and raised the radiate to near 5% silver and higher weight. In 294 Diocletian added to the reformed radiate some good silver, some firm gold, and a larger and smaller low-silver coin. Judging by site-finds, British reaction was to ignore the 274 radiate and the 294 small and middle coin, and instead to continue using the old 1% radiates and Barbarous Radiates. These are the coins that turn up in layers on excavation which are dated by various means from *c*.270-*c*.320.

Hoards cannot be used to construct this picture because in this period many appear to have been restricted to one type of coin. There are hoards of decent coins of the 260s and early 270s; a few with coins of 274-94 – the reformed radiates, which virtually never make it into everyday coin loss on the average site; and after 294 there are hoards of the largest silver-copper coin, sometimes called the follis. The great majority of coins hoarded at this time are poor regular coins and Barbarous Radiates – in other words, the scruffiest end of the scale. It is understandable that after the reforms of 274 and 294, when the 'unsatisfactory' old coinage had been superseded by bright new 'better' coins, people generally chose to bury in one pot either the old or the new, as opposed to a mixture. Because the coins from 274 to about 317 were of considerably higher value than the old 1% radiates and their barbarous cousins, it would not be surprising if the scruffy coins continued to circulate as very small change – rather like my marginal farthings.

So what does this say about that bulge of hoards in the period 260-94? In the first place it is a long period compared with 180-92 or even 238-60. Take into account that the life of scruffy radiates may well have continued until around 320, and the time spanned becomes some three times as long as most of the other early periods. If we were working not on coin hoards (unrecovered) per period, but per year this brings things a little nearer normality. Add to this that, untypically, the bulge of hoards contains largely scruffy coins, low value coins, coins that were dropping off the bottom of the purchasing-power range, and the interpretation changes yet again. These really are not hoards which can be tucked away in the safe knowledge that when the nasty events are over they can be brought out to purchase five new cows. They were probably put away because they could not even purchase one calf, the tax man laughed at them, and even your friendly neighbourhood egg producer preferred a nice ball of your home-produced wool for winter knitting. But you couldn't just throw them away, could you? They might come in useful. The fact that they never did could well account for this epidemic of non-recovery.

Collected information on hoards

We can now go back to look at the table of hoards through time that remained unrecovered from Roman Britain to be discovered and recorded by Prof. Robertson. You may have thought when I mentioned a total of about 1500 hoards that I was being inexact, but unfortunately certainty or even total accuracy in this field is impossible. Even if the total of hoards in the book could be exactly settled it was unsettled the day after the manuscript went to the printers because yet another hoard was reported. But to concentrate on the record in the book is to begin to understand the difficulties of dealing with the actual material as it comes out of the ground.

When there are two pots buried close together, with rather different coins in – perhaps silver or copper, or denarii of around 230 and radiates of around 240 – is this one hoard, or is it two events of hoarding by the same person in roughly the same place? And how close is close? This sort of problem occurs when detailed knowledge of the find is available, and can usually be fairly easily sorted out. You may decide that for your purposes 20 feet between two deposits make them one hoard; further away means more than one. Then, of course, two hoards turn up 15 feet apart, one of denarii buried around 150 and one of copper buried about 350. But snap decisions can be taken, these can be listed, and firm numbers reached.

The real problems come when detailed information is not available. A country parson recorded a hoard of silver coins found in the field of his farmer in 1745. A local squire writing a county history in 1852 refers to roughly the same number of coins in roughly the same area 'on the south side of the road leading out of the village', but makes no mention of the parson and writes as if his hoard was breaking news. Yet one contained 230 silver coins of the early empire and the other 248 coins up to the emperor Hadrian (117-38). 200 coins in the local museum have a find spot in the same village according to a letter of about 1770 which is kept with them. There just are no simple rules for making snap decisions in such cases. The village may have produced three coin hoards, or two, or one. At least we can be certain of one, but beyond that is doubt.

In making the table I made many snap decisions and no other writer would come to exactly the same numbers, except perhaps by accident. Yet the balance between metals and between periods is quite clear and reasonably safe. This is an important point: accuracy is impossible, but useful and reliable information is clearly available. This is not a contradiction in terms, but simply what all scientifically trained people (and many others) know – that every statement contains error, but since in most cases the limits of this can be estimated, the nugget of truth in the centre should be treasured and refined. To the classical mind, to say that every statement contains error is to say that every statement is wrong or untrue: and the wrong and the untrue are valueless. This neatly illustrates the gulf between the different approaches.

Hoards in Britain and elsewhere

Collections of gold coins are the most attractive hoards, but the table makes it quite clear examples, even mixed with silver, are a fairly thin icing on a more substantial silver and bronze cake. The earliest gold hoards sometimes contain British, pre-Roman, gold and this also applies to mixed gold and silver hoards. But with a very few exceptions the British element dies out quite quickly after the middle of the first century AD. Gold hoards almost disappear from sight after the first century, and reappear in reasonable strength only after 364. Hoards of third-century gold coins are rare anywhere in the empire, so Britain is entirely in step. There are two groups of such coins which make a particular point, which are known mounted in jewellery in Gaul and Germany, and in hoards from Denmark – two contexts which may seem abstruse and unconnected, but in fact can be tied together quite usefully. These third-century coins only survive for us to examine because they were trapped during their lifetime. The jewellery coins were taken out of circulation and mounted in necklaces and on rings, and so could never go back into the cycle and be re-minted; this is equally true for the coins in Denmark, which had escaped from the Imperial circulation and got trapped in Barbaricum.

This suggests that the absence of third-century gold coins in casual losses and buried hoards is not evidence of absence of those coins from circulation. The coins were certainly minted; as well as the trapped coins, small numbers survive in museums and collections to prove it. But the great majority of those coins were never trapped. Instead they circulated, were used, went back to the issuing authority and in due course turned into gold coins of the fourth century.

A second set of trapped coins might add to our general picture. Late fourth-century gold appears in decent numbers in Britain, and sometimes in hoards. Those coins, again, did not continue their life in circulation; and whatever the mechanism which led to their deposition it suggests that there were different forces at work in the third century and the late fourth century. Denmark provides another episode rather like the third century, but some two hundred years later in the middle of the fifth century. If you want to study unworn gold coins from eastern mints such as Constantinople struck in the middle of the fifth century, go not to Constantinople but to Denmark, and particularly the island of Gotland. These are deposits of coins which left the empire and settled down instead of circulating. While the third-century coins are sometimes quite worn, which suggests that they trickled out of the empire after use, the fifth century examples are more often in mint condition, which suggests that they were sent straight out of the empire to foreigners. In fact this ties in well with textual evidence of large payments of gold to the Goths of various sorts, to keep them away from the imperial frontiers.

There is another aspect of hoarding gold which needs to be examined here. Previously we have assumed that hoards contain a certain number of coins, rather than a certain value. Of course they vary dramatically, but numbers and value are two rather different ways of looking at it and they do not often

35 *Silver denarius of Julia Paula, first of several wives of Elagabalus (218-22). Early third-century coins are not common in Britain, but denarii occur more frequently than the bronze issues such as the sestertius*

agree. I mentioned earlier the point that if you were a shopkeeper in the late fourth century whose till had mainly copper coins in, and you wanted to buy a gold coin with which to pay your taxes, you had to take 7200 nummi to the money-changer to get one gold coin. That might have meant a bag of 1440 copper pieces, almost certainly not less, in exchange for one piece of gold. It all depends on whether the money was hidden the day before the visit to the money-changer, or the day after the money-changer and before the tax-collector. No one has any difficulty in recognising a hoard of 1440 copper coins – they are rather difficult to miss. But one gold coin is much easier to miss – it might be a brass blazer button – and does not look like a hoard. To extend this one point further, a hoard of 1440 late fourth-century copper coins is almost certainly worth more than the same number of Barbarous Radiates, and this is another factor that diminishes the Radiate bulge of hoards. They may be numerous, but they have very little value compared with hoards of good early silver, or excellent late gold.

The single gold coin, when found, ought therefore to count as a rather large hoard, but for practical reasons this is difficult to put into practice. It does however lead on to a further question, which was raised in acute form when two distinguished French coin workers were considering finds of single gold coins in the west of France. These occur quite frequently especially in the early empire (up to *c*.100), and then again in the fifth century. The first opinion to be expressed was that the presence of these coins showed the economy of Gaul had got off to a flourishing start – so many gold coins buried within only a few decades of the conquest. The second view suggested that gold coins in the ground were not circulating, as they were intended to do, and that exactly the opposite of the first opinion was the case; yes, gold coins clearly got to the west of France, but the poor ignorant natives had no idea what to do with them, and no economy in which to use them, so they just buried them for safe-keeping. A strong verbal punch-up ensued and the workers agreed to differ. If the fifth-century evidence is added to that of the first century (it was not considered in the original disagreement), then I think the balance might tilt in favour of non-use. The first-century evidence by itself could go either way, but since the fifth century is fairly clearly a time of decreasing coin use in France, the increasing burial of single gold coins may be part of that movement.

For the early empire in Britain, that is the period of the silver denarius from the conquest to about 240, the standard hoard contains tens or hundreds of silver denarii. Bronze hoards are reasonably common, but in only one period (41-54) does their number equal silver hoards; and even the smaller number of mixed silver and copper hoards only produces one further example (69-96) of silver being overtaken. This is strange from one point of view, but fairly obvious from another. The former stance comes from comparing Britain with Europe. If you leaf through the French volumes on Roman coin hoards you will find that a majority of early hoards are of bronze, and Peter Guest's work suggests that this is true also in other parts of the mainland (although Germany might have a stronger silver link than Gaul). So in producing a good number of silver hoards and fewer bronze hoards Britain is odd.

Odd, but sensible; if you are putting aside money for the future, then make sure it will keep its value. The case always quoted, and one of the few examples where we have the burying of a hoard well-documented, is that of Samuel Pepys in the 1660s. His position in the Admiralty gave him good warning of Dutch intentions to attack the Thames and burn the British fleet, so he visited all those who owed him money, collected in his debts, always if possible in gold, and buried the result. Being a sensible man he did not do this in the very spot that the Dutch might attack, but took it all up to the house of his father-in-law well away from London, and buried it by night in the garden. There are many points which come out of this, but the one to focus on for the moment is the sense of gathering the most precious coinage in the smallest bulk (in this case gold). So in burying wealth in silver rather than bronze Britain is being sensible.

A hoard of 200 denarii would reduce down to 8 gold coins, but Table I shows that this rarely happens, especially in the second century. On the other hand 200 fairly small denarii would expand to 800 large heavy sestertii or, even worse, 3200 of the most common coin, the as. This is the difference between a decent sized tea-pot and a suitcase; between something which would almost go unnoticed in a coat pocket, and something which everyone would see you lugging to the Blasted Oak in order to bury it. It is the difference between three or four spadefuls of earth, easily dug and back-filled, and a good half-hour's heavy digging to get the case well below ground.

It rather depends on two further factors: how easy is it to collect silver, and how much confidence have you got in the system? It is possible that there was more silver arriving in Britain and Germany than France and Spain simply because of the presence of the army on the frontiers, but not so much in the heartland of the empire. If this is the case then the silver hoards in Britain simply reflect what coins were available. The difficulty of this is that site-finds, which we yet have to look at in detail, are predominantly bronze, whether in Britain or France, Germany or Spain, so the evidence seems to say that both silver coins and bronze coins were present in Britain in the first two centuries. This in turn means that what was hoarded was a matter of choice or common sense.

So why might the older provinces hoard bronze and the newer provinces hoard silver? The form of the question already hints at my suspicions. If coinage is a fairly new thing which has not penetrated all levels of society then it may well be used in day-to-day transactions, but if wealth is to be stored then it should have the intrinsic value of silver, not the system-related token value of bronze. The older the province, the longer coin use has been going, the more firmly it is embedded in the general consciousness, and the more acceptable

36 *Sestertius of Otacilia Severa, the wife of Philip I (244-9). The hippopotamus represents the exotic animals provided for the games to commemorate the Roman Millennium – One Thousand Years of Rome – in 248. Coins such as this, a typical, lumpy, straight-sided third-century sestertius, were never supplied to Britain, although a very few may have arrived in the purses of travellers*

is bronze. This seems to fit all the facts, except that Britain is still devoted to the hoarding of silver – when it is available – in the later fourth century. This time Britain is more or less unique; hoards of late silver are rare anywhere else, although there are a few around the Danube, both inside and outside the empire. By the 380s Britain had been using coins for over 400 years, so the idea of token coinage ought to have taken firm root. In the period 364-411 the balance of 182 hoards of bronze alone and 98 containing a precious metal is unequalled in the rest of the empire – so far as we know at present. There is a lot more comparative work to be done before such statements can be made with anything like certainty.

The bronze hoards in Britain are fewer in the early period, and more in the later period. One hidden factor here is the size of the hoard. In the period 41-54 there are 11 bronze-only hoards compared with 4 consisting solely of silver. The numbers are low and the balance is unusual for Britain. If we look more closely we see that many of the bronze hoards come from excavations at military sites like Usk and Colchester, and vary between 4 and 50 coins. Similar deposits would probably go unpublished if the coins belonged to later periods, because it is so common to find 10 radiate coins in a single pit or rubbish layer. On the other hand, town sites that have been excavated seem rarely to yield 10 asses of Hadrian together in a group. All this suggests that many of the earliest hoards in Britain are casual deposits, lost or mislaid, as compared with the later hoards which are vessels filled with coin buried intentionally for safe-keeping.

The larger, more intentional, bronze hoards seem to occur more in the third century than the earlier period. This corresponds with the period when sestertii were being minted in large numbers and supplied copiously to the Mediterranean area but not to the north-west provinces such as Britain. It seems as if the scarcity of new coin led to the old examples being hoarded. The bronze hoards which end with a few coins of the 260s such as sestertii of Postumus are vital to an understanding of the supply, circulation, and preservation of bronze coins in Britain.

Mixed hoards, as **Table I** shows, were never really popular, whether the coins were gold and silver or silver and bronze. The only point at which they became more common than selected hoards is the last period, when precious metals seem to have been buried without much consideration of the relative contents. Silver and bronze coins together clearly represent more of a mixture than silver and gold, because it is not just the metals being mixed but the whole basis on which the value of the coins depends. This might suggest that mixed hoards were a matter of quick deposition of any money to hand, while selective hoards were the result of a more considered plan of campaign. I would expect the number of coins to say something here, because quick deposits of coins to hand ought to contain less coins than the result of a week collecting in debts in good silver. At first glance this does not seem to be the case, so much more careful work needs to be done.

What use are hoards?

I mentioned above that hoards of bronze coins buried in the third century AD are vital to our understanding of supply, circulation and preservation. This needs to be argued out, together with ways in which coin hoards can be useful other than just as being features in museum cases.

I have fairly violent feelings towards people who write the monetary history of an area of the ancient world – a Roman province or a Greek city state – from the contents of a list of coin hoards. This seems to me a misuse of the evidence, because every hoard is gathered together at a given time, for a certain purpose, and with certain points and principles in mind. All these factors may equate to no more than 'my daughter is ill, I must go and look after the grandchildren, where shall I hide my purse till I get back?' On the other hand they could be 'most of the coins around are of the ruler Dubius; I don't think he will survive the year, and then what will his coins be worth? I had better sort out what I have and bury the safer ones.' Foreign coins may be commonly used in the market place, but normally excluded from hoards: they might even be discarded in the market place as people examine the change they were given, and totally excluded from hoards. This does not alter the fact that there were a lot of them around. Low value coins probably change hands the most quickly and make up a large proportion of each person's money but, as we have agreed, they are inconvenient to hoard. Given these points it becomes quite clear that hoards are a selective sample of the coinage available or in use at the time of burial. They cannot be used as the only guide to coinage and currency in Ruritania.

That said there are two factors which make it worth having a look at any hoard that comes along, sometimes in great detail. Firstly, if the coins had not been around at the time the hoard was gathered or buried they could not have been included. Hoards usually present us with a concentrated sample of certain types of coin. It may be that casual losses never include a certain type of coin, such as the first silver radiates struck around 214-22: reliance only on casual losses to write the story of coin use in Roman Britain would therefore mean that these coins would be left out of the picture. But hoards of denarii buried after 222 do contain these coins, usually in small numbers, so there is absolutely clear evidence that they were available in Britain, even if they got lost in the market place very infrequently. This may be a matter of sheer numbers: the new radiates may have formed one out of a hundred silver coins in circulation, so you need to see 100 casual losses of the period 222-38 to be reasonably sure that the radiates are absent. Virtually no site in Britain has 100 single finds of silver coins of the period, so very few sites have these new radiates. If a site did show 105 silver coins from 222-38 in its finds, I would immediately suggest that it was a scattered hoard anyway – but this may be prejudice against the unusual ever turning up.

The second factor might be value. I suppose I have handled around half a million coins found singly on sites in Britain, and among those there were three gold coins. It would in fact be wrong to say I have handled these three, because in two cases they were removed from the collections by the excavators as being too precious to allow 'other people' to touch. Here again is this strange idea of what is precious; because the coin was gold it was assumed by everyone that it was more so than copper and silver examples. Yet if the coins had been put on the market, some of the copper coins would have reached far higher prices and been fought over much more enthusiastically because a lot of people wanted them, and there were very few to go round. To return to deductions: three gold coins in half a million finds suggests that gold coins were incredibly rare in Roman Britain. A quick look at the hoards shows that though they were never common, there was in fact a fair number around for most of the Roman period. People cared for them, looked after them, and sometimes buried them for safe keeping. If they lost them they put in a lot of effort to finding them again.

It is as a concentration of coins that hoards come into their own. We can start at the very lowest and most difficult end of the scale: if you want to study Barbarous Radiates then nearly every site in Britain that has yielded coins had produced a few, and a prolific site may have produced 50. If your study is to get anywhere you must collect together details of all these coins from every site; photographs, weights, die axes, diameters, perhaps even metal analyses. Fifty here, 3 there, 17 somewhere else, and with a lot of hard work you might gather together a sample of 2000 coins. The Normanby hoard from Lincolnshire found in 1985 had well over 2000 Barbarous Radiates; point made?

So the detailed study of coins is best done from hoards? There are two points for and one against. If the hoard has been saved intact and is available for study, then the whole process is much easier, cheaper, and quicker than wandering round a series of museums and archaeological stores. But the hoard can only be saved intact if someone has the firmness to disregard the usual grumbles of 'why should the local council buy that for the museum? It already has two coin hoards and anyway I have seen this one, and all the coins look the same. Even worse they are not genuine coins they are forgeries.' Powerful points, and, as always with powerful points, very economical with the truth.

It is true that the museum already has two coin hoards, so it has the material to exhibit 'a hoard', and visitors can admire. But museums ought to be places for admiration plus information. For 'Ooh that heap of coins looks exciting. Oh look, it tells you here about where they all come from and how they found out about them.'

The coins are indeed forgeries, or perhaps better, copies, but this means they were made in Britain or close by and therefore represent something local and approachable rather than Roman and distant. The suggestion that they all look the same is at the heart of the matter. I argued earlier that the only two coins that really are the same are those that are struck between the same two dies, head and tail, obverse and reverse, one after the other, and probably in the same morning's work. When you look closely at that hoard are they really all the same? And here is probably a point at which the museum in its initial showing of the coins failed. At a distance of several feet, seen through the glass of a museum case, a hoard of Barbarous Radiates does in fact look all the same. You cannot get close enough to see the detail, and perhaps even if you could, you need someone to guide your first glances.

One may be a rather fuzzy coin, a decent size, quite regular in outline, but strangely indistinct. Another may be a strange slip of metal, nowhere near circular, and with half the design off the flan as a result; but the half of the radiate head that is visible is a superbly crisp little caricature of the official coinage. It needs enlarged photographs and a short text to tell the disgruntled viewer that one is a poor cast of a regular coin (hence the regularity and the fuzziness), while the other is struck from well engraved dies. One is a weak copy of authority, the other is striking (sorry) out on its own. There may be two struck coins which look similar, but not the same as far as the radiate head goes. Their metal may be totally different; one a reddish copper, the other a brassy gold. One has used new metal perhaps from British mines; the other may well have recycled some of those old worn brass sestertii. The struck coins look very like some from the well-known hoard at Worthing – we ought to go to the published photographs of that hoard to check up. And what about continental parallels?

All this is possible, and much more because those Barbarous Radiates have been gathered together for us, so that we can compare one with another on the spot and do a detailed study. Yes, it would be possible to do the same sort of study on the ten BRs from the local Roman villa, but the chances of finding mixes, matches, and misfits is so small. The second good point follows on from this: coins whose life has been brutally curtailed by burial are usually in better condition than coins which have lived a full and happy life in circulation and been buried worn out from constant use. This is not always true – even coins which are nearly rubbish were sometimes buried because there was little more that could be done with them, especially at the end of coin use in Britain. But generally speaking, coins from hoards are in better condition than coins lost casually at the market.

Part of this difference comes from the surroundings in which the coins have spent the last 1500 years. The worst coins I have ever had to deal with, from the point of preservation, were from Roman layers in Winchester which were later covered by the soil and burials of a monastery and the Cathedral. Single coins in layers percolated by juices from decaying bodies do not fare well. Contrast this with the fate of a group of coins of similar composition in a large well-fired jar buried in a mildly alkaline soil. Even if an amount of ground water seeped occasionally into the pot there was little there to start and continue corrosion, and so the coins from the hoard may well have emerged from the pot in very good condition indeed. Of course some single coins from excavation turn up in excellent state, and of course some hoards are in dismal state when found, but the general run of cases shows hoard coins to have an advantage.

The advantage, from our point of view, of concentrating coins of a certain type in a hoard can be taken a step further with the Barbarous Radiates. In looking at the specimens of our hoard we thought that some looked like those in the Worthing hoard, and we were going to check up on this. The fact that we are dealing with hoards means this can be done quite easily, because when hoards are noticed they tend to get studied and published. And if the coins are not run-of-the-mill issues they may well get illustrated as well as described. This means that we can check up not only on whether some of our coins are like those from Worthing or other British hoards, but also on possible links across the channel. This is virtually impossible with single finds or site-finds: they are rarely studied in such detail, and virtually never illustrated. Failure to illustrate is regrettable but understandable from the point of view of effort and cost – and the usually poor condition of the finds. Failure to study brings us back to 'concentration'.

The people in the British Museum coin room who work surrounded by many of the major coin finds from Britain sometimes forget the plight of the single worker out in the provinces who has ten coins on his desk, and no collection at hand to compare them with. 'Why did you not distinguish between radiates from the mint of Cologne and those of Lyon?' Because I only had three worn examples to deal with, and unless you have an enormous amount of experience of handling such coins, you need a reference collection to sort out the details. But if you have a hoard of 500 radiate coins in good condition it is much easier to divide them up into different stylistic groups, and then label one Lyon and the other Cologne.

As we have used Barbarous Radiates as an example of the use of hoards, we might as well stay with copies to make another point. Once you have seen one or two regular radiate coins then there is seldom any difficulty about labelling Barbarous copies. They were apparently never meant to deceive and this is why they are better described as copies rather than forgeries. But at the end of the fourth century, plus or minus 20 years, copying was again in operation; and this time the coins were both precious metal (silver), and so like the real thing that it is only recently that the extent of the matter has been mapped out. 'Why did you not say that one of your site-finds was an official issue and one a copy?'. Because you need a good series of 10 or 20 of both types, and Peter Guest's study of the Hoxne hoard (in process of publication) to distinguish the one from the other.

It was the sheer number of silver coins in the Hoxne hoard, over 14,000, that allowed the first really detailed study of both official coins and copies. This is another example of Unexpected Britain. The old view of Roman Britain deemed it a backwater, in which little high-level culture or valuable materials could be expected. Finds in the twentieth century have changed things, so that when a new hoard of silver or gold turns up on the market East Anglia is one of the first places that people think of as a find-spot. Such large numbers of late Roman silver coins just are not commonly found elsewhere (it would be tempting to say not even in Rome, but that is not where late Roman resources were concentrated. Not even on the Rhine and Danube frontier, would be a more useful comment).

The Hoxne hoard allowed both this material to be studied in detail, and earlier work to be fleshed out. It is now possible to talk with reasonable likelihood of being right about the relative outputs of different mints like Trier, Lyon, Arles, Rome and Milan. To that can be added the ups and downs of supply from these mints to Britain over time; here a flood, there a trickle. And since some coins just do not fit into the official pattern, and sometimes look a little suspect when you have several thousand official coins to compare them with, there are the copies. The regular coins were often clipped, first the bit of silver outside the letters and then the letters themselves, but this always stops short of the emperor himself. When the regular coins and the copies were analysed to find their silver contents the two classes were very much the same: the copies were as good as the official issues, not only in the quality of dies, weight and general production, but even in the metal used. It seems fair to say that since no one seems to have benefited from the production of these copies, they are hardly likely to be forgeries. The simplest explanation (which Peter Guest puts forward) is that they fill the gaps created by the stop-go policy of production at the official mints. This provides an excellent example of what can be deduced from the detailed study of a hoard, but could probably never be done from the examination of individual finds.

The one point which has to be kept in mind in the study of hoards is that they are biased in at least three ways; they were mostly selected from the coinage in use at a particular time for a particular reason and with certain prejudices. They are all very odd hoards, totally untypical of hoards in general, because they failed in their purpose and are still here for us to study; and because they were buried in a specific place at a specific time, it may well be illegitimate to extend information from the study of one hoard to coin use, or even coin production, in general.

This makes them sound a dangerous field of study – and this is true. We now have to go on to think about single finds or site-finds, which fortunately have all sorts of advantages over coins from hoards: but they have their dangers as well.

4 Site-finds

Roman coins found together in glittering shiny masses have an immediate appeal, and people in general are ready to take an interest in them even if they know very little about the times that they belong to. But 50 rather small, scruffy, corroded discs of copper on which very little can be seen at first glance rarely attract attention. There are two steps to getting something out of them, and hence finding something to be interested in. First you need to know what those coins are, how they fit in to the general patterns of both coinage produced by the Roman state, and coin supply to Britain. This tells you what was available to be deposited on any site in Britain; and the first steps towards this come in chapters 1 and 2. The second stage is to find out how the 50 coins under examination compare with the coins from other sites in Britain. Are they the 'right' 50 for a temple, for a site in Kent, for a fort on Hadrian's Wall, and so on? This is the subject under investigation in this chapter.

Lost or binned?

If we go back to the beginning we ought to ask why coins are found on Roman sites. Many comments are made by people visiting excavations, or hearing about field walking, about Romans having holes in their pockets to explain all this money lying about. Such comments can usually be deflected by beginning an explanation of how the Romans did not have pockets, but carried their money in little bags, in bronze purses slung under the arm, or in little metal boxes attached to the belt. 'Where would cutpurses be if people did not have their jingling little money boxes on their belt?' (I paraphrase) asks an ex-slave at a Roman dinner party.

Occasionally the questioner is not to be deflected and comes back to the attack: 'You don't find modern coinage scattered around like that you know'. Well, firstly, are you sure, and secondly have you looked at the finds from excavations to make sure modern coinage is not dug up at the same time as Roman coinage? Modern coinage is certainly dropped and lost but much of it is either swept up by buzzing mechanical street cleaners or, if valuable enough, picked up by the next person to come along. One explanation of the modern failure to lose coins in number might be wall-to-wall carpeting and the disappearance of floor-boards. If you have a solid floor then coins cannot drop between the boards, and if you have fitted carpet you can find

37 *A radiate of Trajan Decius (around 250) is of poor silver – perhaps 30%. The portraiture is good, but the lettering is beginning to splay out and become badly spaced*

the coin you dropped almost immediately. A second point is what happens when a house is removed. If it is Roman and the work is done by archaeologists every morsel is lovingly removed by trowel and carefully examined, so any coin lost in the Roman house is probably recovered. The modern house is removed by bulldozer and JCB, so that there is no hope of finding the few lost coins. Finally, most excavations of Roman sites, even in the countryside, produce a few medieval or modern coins. They may not always be mentioned as spectacular finds, but they do usually get listed in the final report.

When these arguments have been laid out, and the questioner is showing signs of wilting, an honest expert has to admit that a site being excavated in a Roman and modern town may produce a 1000 Roman but only 50 post-Roman coins. It is true to say that on virtually any Roman site Roman coins outnumber any others found; but it is not the case that on virtually any Roman site Roman coins are found in surprising numbers. Why the difference?

Firstly, value. In the modern street you may notice a 1p piece that has been dropped in the gutter, but you will probably pick up a one pound coin. The one pound coin is far less likely to be there anyway, because if the person knew that they had dropped it they would have a good look for it; the 1p could be left without tears. This tendency explains the scarcity of medieval coins as single finds. From the beginning of medieval coinage somewhere around AD 700 until about 1500, the only common coin was the silver penny. It had a high value, and so a peasant household, if they had one or two, would guard them with care. Comparisons are difficult between cultures and from earlier times to the present, but I suspect that the medieval penny was a rather more valuable thing than a Roman denarius. Even if we let them be roughly equal in purchasing power, the problem is solved. The number of Roman denarii and medieval pennies from excavations is not all that different. What complicates the issue is that mass of very low value copper coin produced by the Romans, but totally unknown to medieval Britain.

The playing field is getting a little more level. If we compare the Roman period with a later one then we ought to compare like with like, and if the medieval period is in question, we ought to ignore all but silver coins. But then small value copper coins reappeared in the time of Elizabeth I, and after 1600 there was usually a moderate supply from the mint. There were periods of shortage, but since these were cured by the production of local tokens, that can stand as a general statement. Roman Britain from AD 50-400; Britain from 1600-2000. The periods are roughly the same, but it has to be admitted that although sixteenth-century coins, Charles II farthings, seventeenth- century tokens, George II halfpennies, eighteenth-century tokens and Victorian and modern small change do turn up in excavation and field walking, they never turn up in the numbers of Roman coins on any site. I have not done a careful check, but my impression is that silver of 1600-1920 is almost as rare on sites as medieval silver.

Here we enter an area which has roused strong feelings. Could it be that in the Roman period money was discarded? Nonsense, this is an archaeologist just trying to wriggle out of a difficult question by talking absolute rubbish. You may notice at this point that I have been underhand – almost by accident. I have prepared you to accept that idea of the discarding of useless coins by discussing hoards of demonetised Barbarous Radiates, and my envelope of 30 farthings that I have not yet thrown away. Coins can become valueless apart from their metal content, and scraps of copper hardly count in this respect.

A big objection may come in here from collectors. No coin is valueless; those farthings have a market price well above their face value when they were current coin. That of course would not be difficult, since their present equivalent value is less than a quarter of 1p: but I take the point. If I went round to a collector's shop I should almost certainly get an offer for each farthing, and I might have one or two there with uncommon dates which might take the total above the cost of a decent bottle of wine. Forget it. That is valid today, but it is totally invalid, so far as we know, in the Roman world. We hear nothing of collectors of coins, and nothing of the antique value of coins.

It is possible that there is a reference somewhere to a coin treasured by its owner. I have not come across it, but if it is there I strongly suspect that the value will lie either in the occasion of attaining it – it was given to me by General Tacticus – or something shown on the coin such as a portrait of Alexander the Great. Some coins were handed out on great occasions, and some were definitely kept: the hoard buried at Beaurains, near Arras in northern France, consisted of hand-outs from the emperor stock-piled year by year as the recipient advanced up the State Service. The problem here is that the handouts were in gold – the State Servants wisely declined any token appreciations of their services – and it is difficult to decide whether this was the owner's nest-egg pension fund, or the equivalent of his photograph album: 'Yes, the emperor gave me that one when we got back from recapturing London from that damned barbarian Allectus'. That may sound far-fetched, but the great Arras medallion does have just that picture of the emperor riding up to reclaim London on the reverse.

The only example I can think of in which coins might have been saved for a special purpose is the suggestion made some time ago by Edith Wightman about coins from burials around Trier in Germany. Some burials, probably Christian, had coins of around 317-24, yet the graves contained other objects that did not fit with these dates, and generally belonged to later in the century. The coins themselves were not noted for their long circulation; they dropped out fairly quickly, and rarely occur in deposits after about 335. Wightman's suggestion was that the reverse of the coin explained its long life. When Christians were buried it was hoped that Requiescant in Pace, they may rest in peace. What better added hope than for the motto of the coin Beata Tranquillitas – Blessed Peacefulness (**colour plate 29**)? But we ought to come back down to earth.

The alternative to putting a coin aside because it is special is letting a coin fall by the wayside because it is the opposite of special. Discarding coins may be too harsh a term, for few people will ever actually pick up a handful of coins and throw them out of the window. But there is often a time of sorting, and those coins that fail the test get set aside. The most common example of this today comes the week after a holiday in foreign parts. Pockets and purses are emptied, current British coin goes forward for spending, residual foreign coin is put in a safe place because 'we will do something about that later'.

The Roman experience did not include the instant movement from one currency area to another; in the later empire there was only one uniform currency area. Even if there were differences of economy and coin use in different areas of the empire, they were practised with the same coins. In the earlier empire there was the Rome-centred economy and monetary unit in the West, and the varied and varying provinces of the East. Travel was obviously slower, so that there was plenty of time to change localised money close to its point of origin. The equivalent today would be cycling south from Scotland; for the first day and the night's lodging Scottish notes would probably raise no eyebrow, the same perhaps for the second day, but it might be wise to tender only English notes on the third night. Those who did the journey in comfort on the train might have success with Scottish notes at King's Cross, difficulties at Victoria, and face incomprehension at a garage in Kent. Foreign currency therefore provides little help in understanding the apparent Roman habit of throwing money away.

It is better to seek explanations within the money itself: and modern currencies supply plenty of illustrations. Within a stable currency there is almost always gentle inflation, with the result the lowest coins (such as the $1\frac{1}{2}$p) have slipped off the bottom of the scale of usefulness without falling out of existence.

This is what happened to the Roman system between AD 1-260. But again, direct parallels fail: whereas the recent currencies produced large numbers of small coins, the early Roman system did not. One exception was the pre-Euro Italian currency in the 1960s and 1970s; there small change was rare, eagerly sought after, and substitutes were essential. Most other currencies produced coins for the gas and electricity meters, the slot machines, the telephone boxes, and daily shopping. This is a point at which excavated coins start their course as essential evidence.

The mint at Rome under the emperor Nero struck a whole range of coins from the gold piece through the silver denarius, bronze sestertius, and copper as down to the quarter as or quadrans. The most commonly struck coins were in the middle range, particularly the as. Half and quarter asses were not struck in great numbers, and do not seem to have circulated widely, though some travelled with the army. Very few indeed came to Britain, and this applies to the whole of the period from Claudius (41-54) to around 260. Is this statement true? How can we know?

Well, the smallest coins very rarely, if ever, turn up in hoards – or rarely if ever more than one per hoard. But this is exactly as it should be. When you put money aside for safe keeping you concentrate on value: if anything is to be excluded, it is the smallest type of coin. So far so good – the absence of small change in hoards says little or nothing about whether the coins came in to Britain. But they do not occur as site-finds either. This is significant because what is lost and not recovered, dropped and not picked up, should concentrate on the coins of least value – in fact the casual losses ought to occur in numbers opposite to their value, comprising virtually no gold coins, some silver, more middle change, and most small change. Even the texts suggest this: 'Some people are so mean that they will pick a quarter as out of the muck-heap with their teeth' a freedman tells us, at that same dinner party quoted above. The muck-heap is where the relatively well-off person expects the small change to be – it is dropped, it is not worth scrabbling for, it is swept up and dumped on the muck-heap. But, certainly in Britain, it is just not there.

After about 260 things change The official coins sink in value to something perhaps quite close to that old quarter as, and local copies carry similar values. At this point there is a flood of coin recovery in Britain – a strange way to put it, but let us try to keep facts and interpretations separate. Excavation of a large proportion of Roman sites, or field-walking over them, yields scruffy, low value, radiate coins. Recovery of coins dated after 260 is much higher than any earlier period. On the other hand the purchasing power of coins recovered may hardly rise at all. If the 50 years before 260 give rise to two denarii, then somewhere between 100-200 radiates are needed to equal that.

The number of coins recovered goes up, but the value may not change very much, and with variations according to the standard and size of the coinage this pattern continues through the fourth century up to the end of supply around 400. When low-value copper coins are available in numbers, they are lost in numbers and recovered in numbers.

So in a stable currency system there are two factors which influence the coins that are lost, the coins that excavators and field-walkers recover. The first is the value of the coin dropped, lost or mislaid. The second is the number of coins about. If the mint strikes few low value coins they cannot come to Britain, they cannot circulate widely and be exchanged often, so they will not be lost and cannot be found. There is a fertile field of study here on the numbers of different denominations of Roman coins found and their values. In the early system we know the relationships of each coin to every other. The large brass sestertius is worth four asses – are four times as many of them found? If there are less sestertii than the number of asses then it might be because they are larger and brighter and easier to find in long grass or the fermenting straw of the ale house, or it might be because the number of the two denominations is not equal. On the other hand if there are more sestertii than there 'ought' to be the simplest explanation is that there are more of those coins around and fewer asses. It does seem that there are more denarii recovered than the number of asses would lead us to expect, and it might be that in Britain denarii were passed from hand to hand relatively frequently. This would agree with the surprising number of hoards of denarii in Britain compared with other 'more civilised' areas of the empire.

In the early empire there was a relatively stable currency system, with very limited inflation, so we know what to expect from coin finds and the relationship between different denominations. This happy state explodes in the third century, and almost total uncertainty reigns. A second determinant affecting coin disposal comes into play. All the factors above were made with the proviso of 'a stable currency system': but from *c.*238 the Roman currency system was not stable. This brings in the modern parallel of decimalisation.

When I was putting aside my farthings in the 1940s, my father who worked in the bank would bring home old silver coins that he had extracted from circulation. Bags of silver usually had to be counted, and he would come across a shilling of George III (*c.*1816) or a sixpence of William IV (*c.*1834). Coinage later than 1920 when silver coins changed from sterling (92.5% silver) to 50% silver was to be extracted and set aside anyway. After 1948, when silver left the coinage altogether, all pre-1948 issues were to be extracted. But there was nothing odd about finding the shilling of George III in 1947; it was legal tender, perfectly good (in fact too good) coin, and any shop-keeper would have to accept it. This was because the system had not changed between 1816-1947. After 1920 sterling silver was winkled out from circulation, and from 1948 onwards any silver moved even faster, but earlier coins were still current. The great change came after 1971, when decimalisation occurred, because from that point some denominations were demonetised and if you did not take advantage of the change-over period you were stuck with any odd coins you had. The shilling went on because it became 5p, but the half shilling or sixpence quickly went out. The old penny, its half and quarter went out because of the awkward relationship of 1p = 2.4 pennies. A major casualty was the half-crown, which at two shillings and sixpence equalled a measly 12.5p, and was obviously an unsuitable coin to the tidy-minded. To sum-up, and terminate the reminiscence, a change of system usually leaves certain coins beyond the edge of usefulness, which therefore become prime candidates first for sorting out, and then for setting aside. They are the contents of future deposits, whether singly or in bulk.

So the radiate bulge of site-finds, which in fact mirrors the radiate bulge of hoards, is partly due to the fact that coinage suddenly dropped down to the value needed for buying eggs and a bunch of onions on the market stall, and partly because when they had been used for many years the Great Reform of Diocletian and the later reforms of the fourth century knocked them out of official use. These two factors combined seem to me more than enough to explain the large numbers of such coins that are found today.

In the fourth century, between 294-357(?), reforms of the coinage were common events. The size, weight, and silver content of the base silver copper coins changed at least in every decade, and often more frequently. This became so much a matter for comment that some changes got into the law codes, and certain types of coin were explicitly demonetised. Unfortunately argument rages about which particular types these were, but this hardly matters because implicit demonetisation was happening all the time. What appears in hoards – the good coin – changes at regular intervals. This is why it is so much a matter for regret that the great Coin Hoard volume does not list hoards by their reverse types, which can be dated and set in sequence. The bad coin, the dregs of constant change, went on to the bitter end getting scrappier and scrappier. A few worn out Barbarous Radiates still turn up in the little heaps of copper coin which belong to the last years of the fourth century or the early years of the fifth. This does not mean that such coin was 'current', but simply that it was lingering long after its official life was over.

If we take all these points together it sounds as if we could construct an expected coin list before the excavation has started or the field is walked. There is another way of constructing a coin list before bothering to find the coins, and which ought to be considered. If the loss and abandonment of coinage is the accidental event I have described, guided mainly by the laws of chance, then a long-term view of coin loss ought to give a fairly constant picture. Losses over time ought to even out to produce a steady stream of finds. The ideal coin list from a site ought therefore to be divided regularly through time so that if 350 coins were found there should be one each year, or thereabouts, for each year from AD 50-400. Before objections grow too numerous it is worth pointing out that this in very general terms is what happens in Italy. If the coinage is divided up into the 21 periods used in chapter 1, and a span of 400 years is taken, then very roughly 5% of all the coins found ought to belong to each of the periods. This is more or less true in Italy, with a few periods having a bit more than 5% and a some having a bit less, and of course a certain amount of variation between sites. This is not the picture in Britain.

If we are trying to improve the model of constant coin loss then the first thing to worry about would be what the mint produced. Coins cannot be lost if they have not been minted, and even if they were minted they then need to have been sent to Britain. Times of low minting, such as the reign of Claudius I (41-54), and times of low supply, such as the lack of sestertii in the early third century, will play havoc with constant coin loss.

The second point of concern would be more obvious if we talked about constant money loss rather than coin loss. Do we mean that everyone lost a certain proportion of their money, their wealth or poverty, over time, or a certain number of coins? The two are not the same. A first-century street trader might lose a denarius, one coin. It would be a major loss, perhaps the profit off a day's trading, and this one coin would probably cancel his 'constant money loss' for several years. His descendant in the fourth century would have to lose at least 100 copper coins to stay in the family tradition and fulfil his 'constant money loss' obligations. This will play havoc with constant coin loss. It will also introduce a major factor of uncertainty, because after 260 we do not know how the base metal coinage relates to anything else.

38 *The radiate of Gallienus (253-68) showing a centaur going right has only a silvery sheen, and may have less than 10% silver. The centaur is the badge of the Second Legion, Parthica (LEG II PART)*

Constant coin loss does not work in Britain. A picture of the average site, to which most other sites adhere fairly closely, has major peaks and troughs. Constant money loss is something well worth investigating in the future, but it has so many uncertainties in it that it will have to be done in a very careful and sophisticated way. It really needs a mathematical model, which can be worked out from theoretical principles and then tweaked and improved by testing it against the actual coin finds. Don't worry; I am not about to embark on that here. I throw it out as something which an interested computerist could try in the long winter evenings.

There is another point to bear in mind before we tangle with the actual evidence, one of the series of assumptions which always ought to be highlighted before we get down to the work of interpreting. These assumptions form the main difficulty in communication between people who spend much of their time on the study of archaeological material, and those who take an occasional interest. The occasional interest person will ask a question of the much timer, and be upset when a good answer is not forthcoming. It will depend on the type of much timer they ask whether they are told: 1) 'That's a difficult one', followed by a long confusing mumble; 2) 'But X doesn't imply Y, that's what a lot of people think and it is wrong because . . . '; or worst of all 3) 'That is a stupid question which doesn't deserve an answer'. In fact it was not stupid to the person asking: with the information he had to hand it was quite sensible by any standards. But his assumptions were totally different from those of the much timer. The question therefore appeared to be stupid to anyone with the full set of fully outlined and tested assumptions.

Do we assume that the site was continuously occupied through the Roman period? That is nearly 400 years to account for, and on any scale of values continuous occupation on an exact site for this long is the exception rather than the rule. And if the site was more or less continuously occupied, allowing for periods when it was being rebuilt, 'for sale', left to the married daughter miles away who took years to decide what to do with it, and so on, were the people there using coins through all that time?

There would be a danger here of getting heated, and replying 'You have gone through Roman coinage in lurid detail, year by year, we have agreed the site was continuously occupied, why ask if they were using coins?' Such a reaction however comes from an assumption. There is virtually no household in Europe today which does not have and use coins, however few and however low value; if the Romans had coins, and the farmhouse was occupied, then of course coins were in use. But there is no 'of course' about it. There are many Roman sites which show plenty of pottery used and broken from decade to decade, and not a single coin lost even from the periods when loss was most common elsewhere. It may be that they were very careful households, or that coins were a strange, nasty foreign invention, only used once a year in the tax encounter with authority.

The picture that this involves is not necessarily one of folksy spinning and leather work, with the occasional iron smelting and jewellery making (in other words total self-sufficiency). The once-a-year encounter with coins can take place off the farm. The stock are reared, at a certain point in the year a suitable selection are driven in to market, sold, the proceeds taken to the money-changer, and the silver or golden results taken to the taxman. Any extra can be used to buy stock, seeds, or household goods, even the occasional luxury, in the market. The farmer can return home blissfully coin-free. For the rest of the year other needs and sales can take place through a middleman, who regulates a general system of barter – we supply eggs if you supply new knives when needed. This is a system which most people who work from 9 to 5 each day would consider with horror. They may yearn for this simple life, but it is totally irreconcilable with a daily job which produces nothing useful except money. It is a different way of life, not an optional extra to be indulged in at week-ends; and as such, most people do not have it in their minds as a possible model for Roman Britain.

But it has to be admitted that the absence of coins in a site that has been excavated does not prove that coins were never used on the site. Being really hard-headed, even the presence of coins from an excavation do not prove the use of coins on a site.

> Reality (AD 366):
>
> 'Look what that travelling tinker gave me for that old cooking pan.'
>
> 'He is welcome to it, always leaking. What nonsense is this, discs of metal, demons' work, throw them away.'
>
> Fantasy (AD 1985):
>
> Excavation report by Scribbler and Diggit, p.76
>
> Coins from the excavation were few, but there is a group of eight coins ranging from 320 to 364 from area T2 which show that in the fourth century at least the site was fully integrated into the money using economy of the nearby town and its environs.

By trying to build up a general picture by evening out the travelling tinkers and the money-fearers with the money-grabbers and the tax-men, the presence of coins on a site suggests coin use and the total absence on a site with plenty of evidence of occupation suggests the opposite.

But many sites depend for their dating on the coins found, and this clearly warns of the danger of circular argument. The presence of coins of certain dates is taken to show occupation at certain times, while their absence is seen as indicating abandonment of the site. There are a rather large number of excavation reports which have comments such as: 'There are a small number of coins of the early empire, the earliest of which is of Vespasian (69-79) the latest, Marcus Aurelius (161-80). The next issues are those of around 270. This strongly suggests that the site was abandoned for almost 100 years. In fact by going back to chapters 1 and 2 you can pull this tissue of misconceptions apart for yourself. Bronze coins later than Marcus Aurelius rarely get to Britain. Silver does, but its value means that it is lost far less frequently than bronze. If there were only eight early coins, mostly asses, these add up to half a denarius for 140 years. So one denarius for the period 180-270, 90 years, is not to be expected. The coin evidence is exactly what could be expected and says absolutely nothing about the continuity, or not, of occupation – if you know what is going on in coin supply to Britain and coin use in the province.

The other point over which misconceptions arise is in the relative numbers of coins through time. It is a common mistake to look at the totals of coins in each of the periods and to equate large numbers with flourishing activity on the site and small numbers with stagnation or inactivity. The example above dealt with presence and absence of coins – occupation of the site and desertion; here we go on to degrees of presence. The great problem is outlined in the earlier part of this chapter: early coins are of relatively high face value and correspondingly rarely lost; later coins are of lower face value and are lost far more often. This means that a direct coin-to-coin comparison for practically any site in Britain will show low coin loss up to 260 (the coinage based on the denarius and the as), a sudden burst from 260-90 (the radiate coinage), a diminution after 290 (the reform of Diocletian), and a gradual increase after that as the coinage of the fourth century dropped in purchasing power.

It might seem a great pity that I did not bring these facts from the back of my mind, where they were stored, to the fore in 1963, when I was writing a final coin report for the excavations over many years at the Saxon Shore Fort at Richborough in Kent. The fact remains that I did not, and so I wrote an account of the site based on the coins:

1. The site was a base for the Claudian conquest of Britain and there were many Claudian copies there.
2. After the province had been stabilised the importance of the harbour declined as did the number of coins during the later first and second centuries.
3. The site became important once again around 260 and an earth and timber fort was built. The number of coins after 260 soared.
4. The earth and timber fort was replaced by a stone fort before 290. The numbers of coins remained high.
5. Any fort built in the period 286-96 was a rebel fort belonging to the Emperors Carausius and Allectus. Clearly when Diocletian regained the province for the Central Empire, such holdings would have been emptied, if not disabled. That must have happened because the coins of 296 onwards were distinctly rare compared with earlier issues.
6. The fort was too good to be left to fall down, so the imperial authority took it over and occupation continued to flourish to the end of the fourth century. The coins clearly demonstrate this as they increase throughout the fourth century to a great peak at the end.

The trouble with this is that it fits so well because fact and fantasy have been gently interwoven; if I had realised what I was doing I could probably not have made it so convincing. It was only after writing about Richborough that I decided I should find out more about other sites in Britain, and beyond that, I ought to know what went on abroad. As soon as I had gathered together information from a number of British sites it became clear that the 'Richborough' pattern was simply the 'British' pattern in large numbers.

If the explanation for the bulge of coins after 260 is the construction of an earth and timber fort then every villa, town, temple, village, and farmstead had an identical structure built on it. Put this way, it is so clearly wrong that it is odd that anyone should ever have thought it; but the fact remains that while reviewers picked up other points in the coin report, not a single one saw this mistake. Instead I was allowed to find and correct the mistake myself, which is comforting. The point at issue is that I should not have used an argument based on the history of Richborough for what looked like a particular coin pattern there, when that same pattern was obvious everywhere else if only I had taken the trouble to look.

A single set of information cannot be interpreted without placing it against a background; you must know what is expected before you make a fuss about your discoveries. Thus when you feel a bit under the weather, you may reach for a thermometer; and if it provides a reading of around 37°C you do not phone the ambulance because you know that virtually every one is walking around with the same temperature. If you find it is 40°C you make a fuss (if you still can). People are beginning, 40 years later, to take this point on board as far as coins are concerned, but each time I suggest that this is a general archaeological method which should be applied to the interpretation of all material I am usually met by blank or hostile stares.

The stares may be blank because to gather information from different places and put it together to form a background involves some sort of compression or amalgamation, the finding of averages or the drawing of diagrams, and such ideas and methods are foreign to people who live by words. Most people would be happy with the statement that the number of coins (pots, brooches, barley seeds, pig bones) goes up on every site after 260. They would accept that if your site also showed increased activity after 260 you had no basis for making a fuss about it. The difficulty is that if you express your information in such general terms you lose all possibility of getting further information, because all that can be said is that in this respect your site is normal. Yes, but how normal?

The stares may be hostile because the people have a glimmering of what is involved and they want to publish their explanation NOW: a case of yes, yes, this is all very well but it involves a lot of work, and we haven't got time, so please shut up and don't rock the boat. To which the only honest answer is 'Either do the work and publish a legitimate interpretation, or miss out the interpretation.' This is not a popular response.

39 *Tetradrachm of Diocletian (minted 284-94), struck in Alexandria in Egypt. These coins of copper with a dash of silver have never been found in Roman deposits or on excavations in Britain, but many have been brought back in the last century by travellers and soldiers. (Obverse): The legend in Greek shows the name of Diocletian above the head (**ΔΙΟΚΛΗ** [T]). (Reverse): A female figure standing left, sacrificing over an altar. The L shape to the left represents the year of the emperor's reign – in this case A, the first*

So we have got to the stage where the 56,000 coins from Richborough have been found to be typical of coin finds in Britain – with the one exception of the fact that over 22,000 belong to the last 14 years of the province, 388-402. I have outlined the ups and down in my six points set out above; they can be found, by those who can bear numbers, in the Appendix. The picture was set out in fair detail in chapters 1 and 2. Is this a dead end? Certainly not.

The first sites to get out of the way are those where there is good archaeological evidence of occupation and abandonment, or even a stop-go type of occupation. The most obvious site would be Fishbourne, the Roman palace now open for inspection under a cover building near Chichester. Further west is the Saxon Shore Fort at Portchester which is again well worth a visit, with Roman and medieval walls standing well above head height. Fishbourne comes to an end, archaeologically speaking, somewhere around 290-300. The walls were taken down, the tiles were robbed from the foundations in their trenches and occupation seems to have halted. At Portchester there is virtually nothing on the site, apart from a few bits of first-century pottery, before the 280s. The radiate period is represented but is nowhere near its usual bulge, and the fourth century is well represented, but only up to around 390. If these two sites are compared with one another they are almost mirror images: early at one reflects late at the other. If they are compared with the general British picture then Fishbourne has too many early coins and too few late ones; Portchester, just the reverse.

Other general points come out of simple comparisons. Towns, in general, are different from rural sites. This is obvious in the material sense, for even the Roman town in Britain is a blot on the landscape as large as any until after the sixteenth century. Most of the other sites are smaller blots, with the farmstead or cottage being smallest of all. If these sites have coins then early coins will be far more common on town sites than on any others except for early military sites such as the forts of the early conquest or the later garrisons on Hadrian's Wall, York, Chester and Caerleon. This is not just a matter of numbers – that the more coins there are the more early coins will be among them. A villa might produce 600 coins on full excavation, and this is a fair number to be expected on one archaeological site, such as a demolished modern building, in a town. While the villa might produce 6 early out of a total of 600 coins, the town could produce 60 early coins in the same total.

The difference continues. On both the villa and the town site there will be the usual increase in the number of coins found struck after 260, and on both the coins may go on right up to *c*.400. But the radiate coins will be more common in the town. Not only will there be a lot of them, but they will form a larger proportion of the total than in the villa. In general, and this applies as much to the sites as to the numbers of coins, the villa will have roughly three times more fourth-century coins than radiates, while the town will have about an equal number of the two. The numbers will vary quite widely at different sites, and while many towns obey these rules there are a few that do not. I have in the past called these the Bad Towns, and the ones that follow these tendencies the Good Towns.

This can be taken a bit further by using Verulamium as a Good Town and Cirencester as a Bad Town – or as a Rural Type Town, whichever you prefer. The actual numbers (as always) are banished to the Appendix, and I will try to keep the general comparison to words only. The reason for using these two sites, or groups of sites, is that they start off with very nearly equal numbers of coins found – 9141 for Verulamium and 9981 for Cirencester. From the conquest to 192 the sites are neck and neck; for 180-92, there are 30 for Verulamium and 32 for Cirencester. Then Cirencester moves ahead, providing almost double the number of coins for 192-260 than Verulamium. In the magic year 260 both sites shoot up, but the position reverses; for 260-75 Verulamium has 2000, Cirencester 1000, and this relationship stays constant for 275-94. As always things calm down after 296, but Cirencester goes ahead for the fourth century, with twice as many coins, or sometimes just a few more. Equality is reached in 348-64 when Verulamium at 1162 is more than Cirencester at 1073, but then Verulamium flops to 609 (V) to 1320 (C) (364-78), 11 (V) to 82 (C) (378-88), and a miserable 156 (V) to 1368 (C) (388-402).

Leaving exact numbers out of it there is roughly, sometimes almost exactly, equality up to 200, when Cirencester moves ahead. The position reverses in 260 and Verulamium leaves Cirencester far behind. After 296 Cirencester moves strongly ahead; Verulamium tries to catch up and makes it by 350, but then falls far away after that. I try, sitting writing in Cirencester, not to be triumphalist about this; and one way of being more humble is to ask what these coins mean. We are back to the debris of a vibrant economy versus heaps of old rubbish. In other words lots of coins found by excavation may be the result of market stalls selling goods throughout the day and night, with the consequent loss of small change as it passed from hand to hand. Alternatively, a number of coins may be an index of rubbish piling up in a settlement about to be abandoned.

A quick look abroad suggests that a pile-up of coins in excavated deposits correlates quite well with troubled times in the settlements. Carthage shows remarkably little coin loss during its times of greatest peace and prosperity, from the first century AD to the fifth. Even the take-over by the vandals seems to have caused no great monetary problems. But the brutal reconquest by the Byzantine empire which stripped the area of assets in a remarkably short time led to quick decline, so that there was little left to combat the Arab invasions of the seventh century. The period of major coin loss is in the time of final dereliction and decline. Rome went through a difficult patch in the years 408, 409 (when the city was besieged by Visigoths), and 410, when it was finally sacked. It picked up again quite quickly, but never quite to the same level as before. Coin loss is very high around the end of the fourth and early fifth century. It does not end there, but there seems to be a 'fault' in the coin pattern so that deposits belong to either the 'before 410' or 'after 410' group. This suggests a hiccup in coin use, a major coin loss or discarding, and a re-start on new lines.

If these ideas are quite arbitrarily applied to Britain I tend to see Verulamium as following the Rome pattern, with a crisis demonstrated by major coin loss in the late third century; a lighter pattern continues into the late fourth century. Cirencester and rural sites I would see more on the Carthage line of continuity up to a quick terminal decline. This can be extended to many of the towns of Roman Britain; the good towns follow the Verulamium pattern, while the bad towns – mainly Cirencester, Gloucester and Caerwent – and display the rural pattern. I say mainly because all town coin lists are made up from coins from different excavations at different places inside and just outside the town. If the separate excavations are looked at in isolation then while the total for the town is decisively good, one or two excavations may produce a bad list. Cirencester, Gloucester and Caerwent obviously have one thing in common and that is a position around the upper Thames and river Severn. Exeter, even further west, does not follow this pattern.

The coins from smaller settlements such as villages follow a similar division between east and west, early and late, but with rather less clear dividing lines. The village or small town in East Anglia typically starts off well, grows in coin loss throughout the first two centuries, shows fair loss in the third century but

40 *The celebration of the 1100th anniversary of Rome was in 348. The use of the Phoenix is a masterstroke of propaganda for something which could be seen as the beginning of the end – Rome would only last for twelve centuries. The legend of FEL TEMP REPARATIO announces that the happiness of former times has returned*

then declines in the fourth century. Its counterpart on the Cotswolds shows very little coin loss at all before the mid-third century, and then grows in coin loss through the fourth century, often with a strong finish. While some villages or small towns in East Anglia do go on well into the fourth century, late failures in the West are almost unknown.

The picture for villas is less clear simply because there are so many villas with large coin lists in the Cotswolds and so few in East Anglia. That said, the villa with lots of late coins in East Anglia is an extreme rarity, while it is an expected feature of the Cotswolds. Temples either fail in coin loss in the late third century, or they go on strongly into the fourth. One feature which seems to mark out the coins of temple sites is a large number of the House of Valentinian (364-78) and, in the south-west, of the House of Theodosius (388-402).

As might be expected forts and fortresses reflect the story of their building, use and abandonment. The forts of the Claudian conquest – places like Hod Hill in Dorset or Metchley under the University of Birmingham – have coins of the period up to about AD 60; at this point the forts were dismantled and the sites left open, and so the coin lists stop. The forts of Hadrian's Wall were built in the early second century and most of them continued into the late fourth century – perhaps beyond – and again the coin lists, where we have them, reflect this. The fortresses of Caerleon and Chester are both great early foundations, but they seem to dwindle in the late third and early fourth century. York on the other hand goes right through from the late first century to the fifth. The forts built round the south and south-east coast of Britain, called the forts of the Saxon shore (Brancaster, Richborough, Portchester, Pevensey and others), become part of a fourth-century military system which means that even if they have earlier beginnings (as Richborough does), they go on to at least the middle of the fourth century.

This quick look at different types of site should demonstrate that there is not much hope of linking a certain type of coin loss with a certain category of site. There is a town pattern, but some towns do not conform, and in fact the non-conformist town pattern is the same as the rural pattern of villa and village. But the villas and villages tend to have different patterns depending on whether they are in East Anglia or the south or the west of Britain; the eastern villages are more like the majority of towns and the western villages are more like the general rural pattern. Temples in general have strong coin loss in the later fourth century, but some had come to an end before the fourth century began; and the other category of site to finish strongly is the Saxon Shore Fort which is quite different in function, so far as we know, from the rural temple. Coin loss on a given site is therefore affected by the type of site, the location within Britain, and obviously, by the history of occupation on the site.

I have to admit that this section has been the most difficult to write, because I tend to think now in terms of numbers of coins found at sites of different periods and the profiles that can be constructed to show how the sites differ. But as I explained in the introduction, the numerical approach frightens off many people who are interested in the past. Since I have banished all numbers to the Appendix I hope even numero-timid or arithmophobic people will stay with me if I try to explain the problem that has to be tackled. Its solution, so far, must be consulted elsewhere.

The first two chapters were cast in the mould of the periods within which the coinage was struck, issued, and to some extent used. The coinage found on any site can be split up into groups forming a sequence in time – the coins of Vespasian and family (69-96), Nerva and Trajan (96-117), Hadrian (117-38) and so on. This produces a column of numbers which may add up to 50 coins or 50,000 coins. Clearly there is little point in saying that Trevelgue in Cornwall has 1 coin of Vespasian and family while Richborough in Kent has 386, because Trevelgue has only 67 identified coins in total while Richborough has 50,767. Numbers have to be turned into coins per 100 (percentages) or coins per 1000, and then the two sites can be compared. Trevelgue has a bit over one coin of Vespasian and family in 100, Richborough a bit less. A lot of sites have none of these coins, other sites have 20 coins in 100, so Trevelgue and Richborough are roughly similar in the proportion of coins of Vespasian and family in their lists – but otherwise totally different as settlements of the Roman period.

Beyond that there are two main problems. It has taken a paragraph to compare two sites out of a possible 300–400, in just one of the 21 periods of coin issue and use. How can a large number of sites be compared all through their periods of coin loss? That is the basic question which numerical study has tried to answer. It has taken a long time, a lot of effort, and there is no perfect method or answer. On the way it has been described in almost all possible bad terms – numerical obfuscation is probably one of the kindest. But there is a real subject there, and I urge anyone who can stand a moderate dose of numbers to look into it through the Appendix and the Further reading.

5 The use of Roman coins

We now know all about what Roman coins were issued, which ones came to Britain, how they were hoarded, and how they were lost – but what were they, and what were they used for?

If we are dealing with the whole of the Roman empire then there is a certain amount of evidence; if we are dealing with Roman Britain as an isolated and separate unit then there is virtually no evidence at all. The problem, as always with interpretation, is that it is a matter of thought, behaviour and concepts, none of which can be approached logically through material. You can sit and gaze at the material, commune with it, subject it to stringent statistical analyses, or absorb its vibrations, but none of these, or any other procedures, will lead logically to an interpretation. Once you have taken in what material there is, and where it is, you are free to fantasise; and your fantasies can only be proved wrong, they can never be proved right. The best you can hope for is that they are consistent with the material – unless of course you can find a written source which by definition can deal with thought, behaviour and concepts. This does not mean that a written source is infallible, to be totally believed and applied to every instance: but it does give pointers for consideration.

A strange pamphlet called *De Rebus Bellicis*, literally, 'On things of war', by an unknown author, hence Anonymus, has a section on coinage. It is a pamphlet because it is a short composition produced for a particular purpose; and it is strange because very few such things survive from the fourth century, or indeed from any time in the ancient world. It seems to have been written by someone at a reasonable level of local authority with a fairly wide knowledge of the empire sometime in the later fourth century with the aim of setting the emperor right on a few points of detail. It is just the sort of thing you see today when a new member of a committee goes to a meeting, hears the latest issue of a subject which has been debated off and on for the past two years, goes home and writes a 'little note' to the Very Distinguished Chairman which, in his opinion, will sort everything out. He sends it to the secretary of the committee who reads it, puts his head in his hands for a few moments, and then drops the little note in a drawer. If he is tactful he writes to the enthusiast saying how useful the paper is, that he will draw the VDC's attention to it, but that it would be wiser not to antagonise the man by bringing it up in the near future. It is forgotten and gets duly recycled by the secretary (because the enthusiast typed on only one side of the paper) when he begins his memoirs.

41 *The Roman currency system in use in the first century AD. All the coins date from the reign of Domitian (81-96). Top row (left): Copper quadrans, the quarter of an as; (right): Brass semis, the half of an as. Centre row (left): Copper as; (centre): Brass sestertius, a piece of four asses; (right): Brass dupondius, a piece of two asses. Bottom row (left): Gold aureus, a piece of 25 denarii; (right): Silver denarius, a piece of 16 asses*

The memoirs for some reason hit the headlines, the manuscript is duly left to the Bodleian library in Oxford, and the 'little note' gets preserved for posterity by total accident, while the deliberations of the committee are lost for ever.

These details clearly do not apply exactly to Constantinople in 372, but the principles are there. The *De Rebus Bellicis* got bound up with a pigeon-hole full of documents, the whole batch was copied by a scribe in perhaps the eighth century, and again around AD 1000, to form a manuscript that was itself copied several times in the fifteenth century. Except for one or two sheets, we have lost the copies made before 1400.

We do not know where Anonymus was writing. The fortifications he describes sound similar to Hadrian's Wall, but he is proud of the fact that one of his ballistas, or catapults, can shoot bolts across the Danube. Even that is little help either for the exact location or the performance of the ballista. You can jump over the head waters of the Danube in south Germany; on a clear day you can just see across the delta of the Danube as it flows into the Black Sea.

The matters which concern Anonymus are faults in the coinage. He goes through an imaginary history of coinage which he thinks started with gilded leather discs, and he reaches his own times when too many gold pieces were base copies. The fact that he solves the problem by putting the mint workers on an island suggests that he thinks that genuine dies were being used out of office hours to strike the gold plated solidi with copper cores that are known today. But his main contribution to the use of coins comes in two different sections; a set piece on the dangers of squandering gold in official hand-outs, and a total throw-away opinion that coins are produced for buying and selling (emendi et vendendi utilitas).

The official hand-outs were the distribution of gold and silver coin to the army and other state officials on certain annual occasions and special events. I mentioned above the Beaurains hoard of gold and silver coins, and compared it to grandfather's photograph album, because the coins and medallions in it form a record of state service handed out by the emperor, or a high official, to one man. Anonymus points out that though largesse, the scattering of coin, is an essential part of the emperor's benevolence, he could get the same benefits by handing out the same number of smaller coins, and so save the state a large amount of bullion. The recipients, including the army and state servants in Britain, would have reacted badly if this document had ever been made public, or if the word had ever got out that the emperor was considering this course of action; the hand-outs were what was left of their wages. The wages, stipendium, had not kept pace with inflation in the third century and the administration had taken the short cut of providing goods to the army in kind. So instead of getting wages, and then buying things with them, the goods were supplied direct. Obviously the soldiers would not continue to serve purely on the basis of board and lodging, even if drink were included, so there was a regular habit of imperial benevolence. Put more bluntly, after the soldiers and state servants had been clothed, fed, kept warm, and given a little pocket money, there was a regular handout of silver and gold to make up for the fact that there were no regular wages.

There is not much to say about the throw-away line – for buying and selling. That is the Anonymus's view of coinage, and in the fourth century, when exactly the same coins circulated in very similar numbers throughout the provinces, it is reasonable to take it as a view which could have held in Britain.

There are two other written sources which can be scoured for hints about coin use. Each is set in a firm local context miles away from Britain, one in Palestine and one in Rome, but both are from the years AD 30-70. They are at opposite ends of the social, and moral scale. The first three gospels, Matthew, Mark and Luke, form the lower end of the social scale and the upper end of the moral; the *Satyricon* written by Petronius at the court of Nero is clearly the exact opposite. Yet there are similarities which make some points fairly certain, and there are differences which seem to be due to the contrast between the centre and the provinces.

Unfortunately the gospels suffer from translation. The New English Bible is a bit better than earlier translations in this in that it often tries to avoid making silly statements about money, but it can slip badly in this process. A king decides to call in his debts and starts with a man who owes him 10,000 talents – this is translated as 'millions', and a footnote mentions the talents; this is excellent. But then that man tries to pay by calling in his own debts and starts with someone who owes him 100 denarii. This is given in the footnote, but the text has 'a few pounds'; this is total nonsense.

The main key lies in the workers who are standing in the village square early in the summer day hoping to be hired for at least a day's work. The farmer comes out and hires some of them, agreeing to pay them a denarius for a day's work. He comes out at lunchtime and does the same, agreeing to the same wage, and so on. Since this is a major foundation for understanding, or perhaps interpreting Roman coinage, the first question to ask is – can we trust it?

There are lots of avenues for possible doubt here. First of all, is the text reliable, does it really represent what was said in the first century AD, or is it a much later invention? As far as I can see the written sources make it quite clear that the text, in Greek, as we have it today was certainly settled by the late third century. All the early manuscripts agree on the wording – something by no means always the case – so the previous generation of manuscripts in all areas in which the Christian church was established were following the same text. This takes us back into the second century, two or three generations after the first manuscripts were produced, and we can get no further. It is perfectly possible that parts of a set of memoirs of the man called Jesus were tidied up after his death by a group of well-wishers who were set on world domination, but, if so, this is one of their most unsuccessful attempts. Tidying up should have made obscurities clearer and unacceptable statements more bland; as this parable stands it does neither. It is subject to a whole range of contradictory interpretations, none of which is bland. I can see no reason at all to doubt that it formed part of the record of Jesus from an early date.

So, if it seems reliable as a text, is it a sensible statement? We know how vague Good people can be about money; is this just another example? Here Jesus seems to be addressing his immediate followers, but elsewhere he is talking to crowds of very ordinary people surrounding him. 'We all have our little nest-eggs hidden away for when we need to buy a retirement cottage' – a spiritual bishop might be able to get away with a silly statement on money to an audience of landed gentry, or society ladies, but he may be hooted at if he does the same thing at a Miners' Gala. What Jesus said seems to have appealed to the people in the street, and the disciples were quite capable of asking questions if they doubted his statements. If he said a denarius for a day's wage that is unlikely to have been far wrong – for a whole day's work. But you can sense the disapproval growing as the farmer goes out at midday and offers a whole denarius for half a day's work. That is not fair; and to do the same in mid-afternoon is plain silly. The afternoon wage cannot be obviously silly unless the whole day's wage was fairly sensible. And the point about the references to coin in the gospels is that they fit very well together. Either someone has been over them, very early on, and tidied them up, or they made good sense at the time they were first said.

We might try a quick glance at Diocletian's Edict on maximum prices and wages to see if things tally. This is difficult because the system of coinage had changed dramatically, and so the only way forward seems to be through bullion, silver and gold, which seem to have kept their purchasing power fairly constant. An agricultural labourer, or a sewer cleaner or a camel driver, gets a maximum daily wage of 25 denarii. These are units of account, not coins. They may be represented by the large copper-silver coin, called the follis, and it may be that four of these coins equal one silver piece of perhaps 100 denarii – I apologise for the ifs and buts, but they need to be remembered. Let us talk of a silver piece. The gospel farmer was willing to pay a labourer one silver piece for one day's work; the camel driver expects one silver piece for four or five days work. But there is a big difference: neither sewer cleaning nor camel driving are peak-time activities, they go on throughout the year. So one day's work can be paid at a lower rate than the peak-time grape harvest. Additionally, the worker can expect daily employment throughout the year, whereas the agricultural labourer may be very lucky indeed to get one day's work in three. The check suggests that things are not too far adrift.

42 *Denarius of Tiberius (14-37) which circulated during the life of Jesus Christ. This type of coin is often referred to as the Tribute Penny shown to Jesus when he was asked whether it was proper to pay taxes to the Romans. This is possible but unlikely; issues minted in Rome were in a minority among silver coins in Palestine early in the first century AD*

Back to our debt of 'a few pounds', derived from 100 denarii. This represents the total wages of 100 working days, and that is as much work as you might get in a year. A year's wage – not a year's savings, but the basic take-home pay. This does not make sense today unless it is translated into thousands of pounds. Even the old age pension in Britain in 2002 is several thousands of pounds a year, and you cannot go much lower than that and still survive. Perhaps this is how we should work. Give the labourer, his wife and three small children, the old age pension at least: this makes each denarius about £25-30 in the money of 2002.

Cut to 'The traveller who fell among thieves'. Rescued, he was taken to an inn by a Samaritan (a foreigner, a heretic of all people), who went off having given the inn-keeper two denarii and saying 'look after him; if you spend any more I will repay you on my way back'. Bed, breakfast and evening meal for two or three days for two denarii. The total bill ought not to be as much as a day's wage, or no one could ever afford to work away from home. On the other hand, if living away from home is not counted as extra and added to the wages, you will make very little out of your work. So three day's board and lodging, perhaps extra food, and ointments and bandages, for two day's wages, for about £50. That is a good bargain today, though it is within the realms of possibility if you are well outside the expensive areas of Britain. Any adjustment needed to make the gospels more credible will be minimal.

Other statements about denarii begin to make more sense. The woman who lost one lit the lamp and swept the house out till she found it. She had mislaid a £20 note at least. The disciples are horrified at the idea of feeding the five thousand – 200 denarii would not buy the bread to feed them. 5000 people at £1 a time for a decent very basic meal mainly of bread, the only meal of the day: 200 x £25 = £5000. Mary Magdalene breaks a pot of precious ointment worth 300 pence and pours it over the feet of Jesus. The New English Bible suggests 30 pounds, footnote 300 denarii. Some present said, what a waste, the ointment could have been sold and the money given to the poor. At 300 pence that is a bit penny pinching; at £300 it is getting serious; at the true value of £7500-8000 you are tempted to wonder.

Meanwhile back in the Temple the widow is putting dua minuta, two minuta into the poor box because that is all she has. What are dua minuta? St Mark comes to our aid (since those are Palestinian coins and the gospels are going all over the empire nowadays): he comments Dua minuta quod est quadrans, for the benefit of readers in Italy. Two minuta make what you know as a quadrans; a quarter of an as, with 16 asses to a denarius. Divide our £30 denarius by 4 x 16 (64) or 60 to make it easier, and she had managed to save 50p from her old age pension this week, but hopes to do better next week by cutting down on the gas fire as the weather is getting warmer.

If she saved up the money until she had an as, £2, four weeks saving for her, she could buy two little birds like sparrows, for a celebration lunch when her old sister came to visit her. This is according to St Matthew. If she were even luckier she might get the special (St Luke) rate of five little birds for two asses, a dupondius. But to take advantages of reductions like that you have to save for eight weeks. Two starling drumsticks could be tasty, if hardly filling.

This is all very well in Palestine, the provinces; what happens in Rome? Our text here, the *Satyricon* of Petronius, Trend Setter (Arbiter Elegantiae) of the court of Nero, has its own set of problems. No one doubts that the text is real, but there is considerable difference of opinion as to how much of it we have and what on earth it is. An anti-hero and associates lurch from disaster to disaster somewhere in south Italy and north Africa. The text appears to break off every so often and bits may be lost – or that could be how it was written. One inspired commentator suggests that it is a Daily Fable of the life of Lowly Folk, designed to be read out at court amid gales of laughter at how those ex-slaves do behave. Clearly we have to be very careful what we take for granted, but certain points can be made.

If you are going to make people laugh then your comment has to be on the laughable side of normality. If it is way out there is nothing funny about it; if it is an exaggeration that itself can be laughable, if you have nothing else to laugh about. If you make two statements, one an exaggeration, one a reduction, about the same sort of thing then reality has a good chance of being somewhere in between. This is just what Petronius does, and luckily for us it concerns denarii and food. The point at which most coin references occur is a dinner party given by a rich ex-slave or freedman, to his less successful cronies. The anti-hero and associates get invited and spend a bibulous evening. As nothing too explicit in the way of sex happens here, this Cena Trimalchionis (Trimalchio, the freedman's, dinner party) has been a set piece for Latin texts for some time: the rest of the work is rarely offered.

In section 45 a crony is complaining to a fellow-diner that he has to go off to a dinner the next night as well. He is not looking forward to it, but it is a matter of duty. He can take his family, but they will only be fed at the two denarius a head rate. That is pretty basic, is it really worth the trouble of going? This sounds to us, reared in provincial Palestine, disgraceful. Turning your nose up at a dinner costing £50 a head? This must be part of Petronius's high life – he clearly has no idea of how the masses feed. Yet in section 79 Trimalchio boasts that he gave a dinner not so long ago to anyone who liked to turn up that cost him two denarii a head. That's what Trimalchio calls munificence – and I think the point is to pause and wait for the gales of laughter in the court at the idea that two denarii a head provides a posh dinner. So Petronius is caught between doubt at whether a two denarius dinner is worth turning out for, and pride at giving a two denarius dinner. We are well above subsistence level either at the court, or even in Trimalchio's house, so the idea of £50 a head in Rome may be near the truth. It sounds a lot, but is it expensive for a hotel wedding reception?

That would mean a good meal in London for three days' bed and breakfast in – no, there is bound to be a reader there who will get upset, let us just say the inexpensive provinces. We have agreed that £50 for three days' bed and breakfast is possible, but a good bargain. I am afraid that we have to agree that in the sort of London restaurant Trimalchio would choose, dinner might well come out at £50 a head. It is all horribly plausible, although the gospels become uncomfortably communicative, and the *Satyricon* gains in snobbishness. In each case the move from blandness is in the right direction.

If we go further with Diocletian's Edict, even remembering that the prices and wages quoted there are maxima, a cloud appears on the horizon. Daily wages – farm labourer, with maintenance, 25 denarii: ¼ (?)of silver piece, ¼ of £25, £6, ?£40 a week, £2,000 a year. Clothes guard – for each bather – 2 denarii: ?50p. A prod or whip, turned, 5 denarii: ?£1.25. Six pounds of cut grass, 1 denarius: ?25p. That is part of the cloud – the prices quoted, even at the lowest end of the scale, make the wages seem totally inadequate.

The other part of the problem is formed by the coins themselves. There probably is no 25p piece – one denarius. There may be a 50p piece (2 denarii) and a £1.25 piece (5 denarii) – but the 2 denarius piece is almost unknown in archaeology, certainly in Britain, very likely in France, and I have seen none and heard of few in Italy. The radiates, possibly 5 denarii, £1.25 pieces are fairly common in the Mediterranean but rare in Britain. The folles or nummi at 25 denarii (£6.25 – £5 note) are not commonly lost anywhere, but they do occur from time to time.

The wages are totally inadequate to buy the goods listed in the Edict, the coins are almost irrelevant to the simple process of buying weekly supplies on the market stall, in fact the whole thing is a mess. There are various possible reactions. First, this whole idea of giving a modern value to ancient coins is pointless not only because it is so unsure, but worse, because it results in hopelessly inflated values. These points may well be true, but there is a consistency which I think needs to be considered. The idea that the values are hopelessly inflated might be expressed by the unwary as follows – 'Really! A wooden prod or whip £1.25 – ridiculous. That is the sort of price we would have to pay today. We are talking about a society in the dim and distant past, one that has only just come up out of barbarism in the case of Britain, and you talk as if they had been using money for centuries! This is bad 'they were just like us' nonsense.' A pungent statement of objection, and a useful indication of a dilemma.

I resolve the difficulties by putting all the problems into one package. The absence of the smaller coins in the archaeological record, particularly in Britain, must be an important point. It is backed up by the presence of a few larger coins, the folles. Coins were used and lost, but not at the market stall level. This suggests either that market stalls did not work on coinage, but in some form of exchange, or that provincial Britain had its own 'minuta' like Palestine in the first century AD. Either the world of coin use was way above the level of the household economics of the agricultural labourer (with maintenance), or the Barbarous Radiate eased the exchange problem. If the Barbarous Radiate was rated at four to the denarius, we have got down to a 5p piece and there is at last a way to buy a single egg.

My feeling is that this is clutching at straws for two reasons. Since the minutum in Palestine in the first century was only half a quadrans, 25p, I have doubts about pieces smaller than that. The Barbarous Radiate might equal the Palestinian minutum at one denarius. The second point is more a reason and less of a hunch. *If* the Barbarous Radiate had this low value, what had there been before to prepare the way, and what came after to follow up the demand which such a coin might clearly create? There is nothing coin-shaped to fill this need.

I therefore assume that constant coin use operated at land-owner, farmer and shop-keeper class, but below that coins were mainly needed for relations with authority. When David Walker studied the great deposit of coins from the Sacred Spring at Bath, he calculated by very dangerous methods that there might have been about 2 sestertii per person in Britain in the middle of the second century AD. This might have been a total of eight asses, or the occasional use of a denarius, or a constant hold on two large brass sestertii. He was wrong. Of course he was wrong: the odds against him being right are overwhelming. But he was absolutely right to try the experiment of working it out, and he may not be more than 200-300% out. He said as much himself, so there was little point in colleagues getting extremely het up about it all. The value of coins available for each person in Roman Britain in about AD 150 probably lies between 0-30 sestertii. This was calculated from what was produced and supplied, not from what has been lost and found.

If I can be blunt for a moment, anyone who reads that last paragraph and writes somewhere that Reece says that in 150 each person in Roman Britain had about 15 sestertii – halfway between 0 and 30 – is an idiot who should never be allowed to use any numbers ever again. We are dealing with errors which might cancel each other out, or may add up alarmingly; with doubtful assumptions and dodgy calculations; we are dealing with probabilities and possibilities and all these must be understood and quoted. We are working in the sure and certain knowledge that we are not right, in fact we are wrong. So we should press forward to improve our guesswork.

The point at issue is that all the evidence, firm and doubtful, useful and dangerous, points to the view that coins and coin use were not universal, certainly in Roman Britain, before the early fourth century. The coins are not there, and their values are skewed way above the needs of the farm labourer wanting basic food. The values and prices that we know from written sources might just be relevant to wage-earners in Mediterranean enterprises, but seem totally unrealistic for the shepherd on the Cotswold hillside. At some points in his life that shepherd has to pay taxes for himself and his family, unless the person he works for takes that over as part of his 'pay'; therefore he must save up coins, or sell something to satisfy state demands. But I suspect that the coins come and go in his life at given times in the year and with little relevance to the daily life of his family.

Before leaving the anecdotes and trying to fit the ideas together to form an outline of how coinage might have appeared to a middle-class Briton, we could look at the charge levelled earlier that Britain in the later first century was just emerging from barbarism and that civilised money usage, which means high prices, was way in the future. In the first place the label of barbarism is a means to mark off the user of the label from the recipients. Rather worse, the modern sense of the term is not the same as the Roman usage. The barbarians were people outside the empire who were unfortunately not under proper control, and not subject to taxation. Some of them had the undesirable habit of moving round from place to place. But they were knowable and known; traders moved among them, their languages were recognised, and some of them came into the empire to work. They were different but were real people. Beyond them, further out from the frontiers, were the real outsiders who were so hazy that there was not even a generic name for them. If a map had been drawn, then outside the frontiers would have been the worthy foes, duly labelled 'barbarians', but beyond that the simple statement 'Here be savages'.

In the second place Julius Caesar had been over to inspect the Britons in the 50s BC, and some sort of relationship had started with the Roman state which probably continued for the next hundred years. John Creighton has suggested that sons of the tribal worthies went to Rome to be educated and polished; he sees evidence that this process was successful in the coinage they issued on their return, in the very early years AD (it would be interesting to know how difficult they found the culture change from aristocratic life in Rome to wooden palaces on British estates). Like their fathers and sometimes perhaps mothers, they produced gold, silver and bronze coinage. Was the temptation on returning from Rome to hand out coins in the Roman way? We know nothing about this at the moment, but continued study of finds of British coins and the contexts in which they were deposited may fill in the blanks.

After AD 43 the Roman army appeared with a very non-British way of life. They herded together in forts, 100 to the acre (0.4ha), using foreign types of pots, importing foreign food-stuffs and ways of food preparation, and they were paid at the flat rate throughout the empire. There may be a parallel here with the arrival in a developing country of a supposedly liberal-minded multi-national company who cleanse their corporate conscience by paying the local workers the same as they pay workers in the rest of the world. I have decided that this is bad; they ought to pay the workers the local rate, and add the balance to the education and health budget of the whole country. Whatever the rights and wrongs, the provision of international wages certainly must create confusion in the developing economy. The worker coming out of the factory gates can buy a chilled can of drink at British prices, while the villager who sells a little produce off his small bit of land to keep himself and his family alive regards such sums as riches. Yet if the factory workers can pay a high price for vegetables, why sell at a lower price to anyone else? Gradually the general price level must rise towards what the incomers are able to pay.

The government agencies, from the governor downwards, will probably pay their employees at the imperial rate – or perhaps they will use the imperial rate in book-keeping, and pass on a half to the employees who at first know no better. But gradually such siphoning-off of surplus will decrease. Traders who purchased goods in southern Gaul and brought them to Britain could obviously not sell them for less than they paid, and they had to add on the cost of travel. Any imported goods must have sold at foreign prices. With a steady price gradient from Italy through Gaul and Germany to Britain things must have evened up fairly quickly. If the Germans had to pay southern Gaulish prices for what they imported, why should the British pay less if they made other things and sent them to Britain? And all the time the state servants, military or civilian, had the same money that they had in Italy and could probably not argue if the same prices were charged.

Finally there was the currency system which was constructed for Italy by the emperor Augustus, and had settled down to Italian and nearby needs. It may be that at first the coins were too high in value even for the shop-keepers and land-owners. This happened when the British moved in to Malta around 1800, where the whole system of coins they found was based on the coinage of the Knights of St John, scudi, tari, carlino. British coins were brought in and given Maltese equivalences, but there were Maltese coins and values below that of the British farthing. Obligingly the royal mint struck subdivisions of the farthing which were pointless in Britain, but used in numbers when sent to Malta and the West Indies. This did not happen when the Romans moved into Britain and it seems likely that money-using was allowed to creep up to meet the value of the coins available. While today some bed and breakfast houses are cheaper outside London, the scale of values overlaps, and there are some pricey places in the provinces – perhaps for no better reason than that Londoners sometimes stay there.

Early gold

If we keep our equivalence of a day's wage, a silver denarius, to roughly £25 in Britain in 2002, the gold aureus becomes a thing of awe: at roughly £600 it is not really a denomination that can be spent in a shop, but more like the holiday money saved up for the year. This agrees with John Kent's dictum that a solidus was rather like a traveller's cheque – a way of carrying valid money around with you which could be cashed in to pay expenses. He always insisted that a gold or silver coin could not be spent, if by that you mean handed over and change received. I have always repeated this, but I have never found the ancient justification for it. A complication arose in the later empire when the movement of bullion across provincial boundaries was outlawed.

The Kent doctrine fits in with much that we know and feel about gold coinage. Perhaps the most important point is that if you can buy something worth less than a gold piece in a shop and receive change, then you and the shop-keeper are doing the official money-changer out of his rightful perks. His job is to have state gold and silver for sale, and to hold stocks of state bronze to hand out in exchange for bullion. As the precious metal comes in you will get the official rate in bronze. If you want the gold or silver you not only have to supply the official rate in bronze, but you have to pay extra for the transaction. Thus a denarius handed in will gain you the proper 16 asses; if you go with asses to get a denarius you may need 17 of them.

There is also a sense that gold and silver belong in some sense to the emperor and you receive the precious metals on loan, with the undertaking to pay them back in due course. Not so much the value, for repayment in copper would not be acceptable. It is not the value that is part of the emperor, but the actual gold and silver which is somehow sacra, sacred, set apart. His, because he is sacra, but definitely not yours because you most certainly are not.

Finally the anti-hero of the *Satyricon* can be brought in, on his travels with a few gold pieces sewn into the seams of his shirt – just like traveller's cheques in the body belt. But what happens when he went to the baths? He handed his clothes in, the attendant guards them for the maximum two denarii specified in Diocletian's Edict, and a shirt is handed back which is not only not his, but is now without the added value. Later, in a tight situation when he is likely to be arrested on a serious charge of killing a witch's goose by which she tells the future, he throws caution to wind and gives her a gold piece to escape justice with the words 'With that much you could buy not only some geese, but the very gods themselves'.

Aurei did come into Britain, as a few hoards tell us. They probably concentrate in military areas, but there is a danger here of labelling the site military because of the gold coin or hoard. They were virtually never lost for the most obvious of reasons. They are the stuff of wealth and high finance, and as such their everyday role in Britain must have been fairly limited.

Early silver

We do not as yet know much about the supply of silver to Britain. There is no doubt that it arrived, circulated, was used and lost, was hoarded, and that most of it left the province again in the tax returns. What we could know about it will appear later under the heading of bronze coins. Richard Duncan Jones suggests that there are differences in the denarii that turn up in hoards in different provinces; but how this happened, and for what proportion of the coinage it is true, we do not know.

I suggested in an earlier chapter that the number of denarii lost in Britain was higher than should be expected if it is assumed that coins would be lost in roughly opposite numbers to their values. The least valuable coins would be lost most often, the most valuable would be rarely lost. This works for gold, and will be examined for bronze later. At the moment we can look at the numbers of bronze sestertii and silver denarii lost on sites in Britain. Some work of 30 years ago (which has not yet been updated) suggests that from the conquest to AD 100 denarii turn up as casual losses more often than sestertii. Around AD 100 for coins of Trajan (98-117) there are about equal numbers of the two denominations. The sestertius predominates in the second century by about 5 sestertii to 1 denarius, and then after 200 there are denarii but no sestertii.

There is a major fault in the way this has been expressed, but I can do no better for the moment: I will look at the problem in more detail in the section on the archaeology of coins below. For the moment it is enough to point out that what I have quoted is the date at which the coin was struck. The only information that this gives on the date at which it was lost is to provide a starting point – the coin cannot be lost before it is struck, but it can be lost at any time after, even up to today. What the figures might represent are not losses but supply: if as many denarii of Trajan get lost in Britain as sestertii, then it could be that equal numbers of the two coins were supplied. Even this is probably wrong, because while denarii circulate – come in to the province as pay and leave it as tax – sestertii stay put. Once they have been supplied no one outside the province is interested in them. A proportion of denarii supplied to the province get lost there; loss may be the fate of a majority of sestertii.

These quibbles had to be put down because they are major points in any subsequent argument. But the equality of denarii and sestertii of Trajan in site-finds is made more surprising by the quibbles rather than less. Yes, they were not all lost at the same time; and yes, their numbers might be linked to supply rather than a given date of loss. But even so if most sestertii were in fact eventually lost in the province, and only a proportion of denarii met the same end, then the balance between the denominations is even further from the simple theoretical model. Denarii are worth four sestertii, so one denarius should be lost for every four sestertii. Equality of losses suggests a remarkably higher number of denarii either supplied, or in circulation, than might be expected.

In hoards there is a much more even change. Mixed bronze-silver hoards are usually small compared with the major deposits of silver. These grow in the number of hoards found through time, with variations, but more obvious is the growth in the average number of coins in each hoard. To some extent the lowering of silver content is to blame, but this would only account for a

43 *The decline of the currency system between about AD 1-260, as shown by the sestertius. Clockwise from top left: Augustus c.AD1; Domitian c.85; Commodus c.190; Postumus c.265; Severus Alexander c.230; Hadrian c.130; Nero c.65*

doubling of the number of coins between AD 50-200. Greater wealth seems to be being hoarded – or rather, as we ought to say, buried and not recovered. A hoard of 300 denarii is not too unusual, and this figure has already turned up in the gospels as precious ointment to the value of £7500. There were people in Britain, a bit later than Mary Magdalene, who could have bought that ointment instead of burying their coins.

Early bronze and copper

To start with, copper coinage was a major problem in Britain. The army was presumably being paid in silver, but that was useless if there was no change for the £25 note. The natives did have their scrappy bronze coinage, but who in their right minds would accept scruffy British coins as change for a solid silver, completely official Roman denarius? There were no reserves in the treasuries, which dealt with treasure rather than scrap metal. The mint was for some reason impervious to pleas for change and did virtually nothing, so there was little new coinage to send out to Britain even if anyone had thought of it. The few regular coins that arrived were copied with some sort of discipline as to size, weight, and even metal, but often with more enthusiasm than classical art.

This bad beginning was little more than a mild aftertaste by the 70s AD when Nero had minted large numbers of copper and bronze coinage and sent a lot to Britain; and Vespasian and his family had established minting and distribution on what seems to have been a regular basis.

So what did this seemingly regular basis consist of? Early copper coinage is one of the bright spots of coinage in Britain, due mainly to the work of two people. David Walker studied the 12,000 + coins from the Sacred Spring which feeds the Baths and Temple complex at Bath; and Andrew Hobley worked his way round Europe finding out just which bronze coins between the reigns of Domitian and Commodus settled in which areas. It is only fair to say that neither of them started out totally from scratch, there were all sorts of ideas and suggestions floating around for some time before their work; but in each case they did large amounts of new work and knocked the subjects into shape.

It had been suggested that the asses produced by Antoninus Pius around 154-5 with Britannia sitting on a heap of stones on the reverse was a particularly British matter (**18**). This was not because of the image – Hadrian had issued several types of coin showing Britannia and they seemed to turn up anywhere without rhyme or reason. In contrast the coins of Pius seemed to be concentrated in Britain. Was this a case of an issue from Rome sent out to the province, or was it local manufacture? One suggestion was that this particular issue had rather lumpy misshapen flans, even if the cutting of the dies seemed to be orthodox. This might have meant that the dies were cut classically in Rome, but the coins were struck provincially in Britain. I was unhappy with this idea after I tried the experiment of taking a tray of copper coins of Antoninus Pius, turning them all head upwards, and asking friends to select the lumpy coins with the Britannia reverse. This seldom produced any clear results. Yes, if you saw the Britannia you agreed that the flan was lumpy, but if you selected the lumpiest flans they were not always Britannias.

Walker started his detailed work on the Bath coins by looking at these Britannia issues to try to resolve the argument. He found a lot of die-links; many of the large number of these coins at Bath had been struck from the same dies. This is not commonly found in a sample of coinage which has circulated throughout the empire, for the simple reason that the products of one morning's striking in the mint may have been distributed in batches to various places, and moved round a lot after they arrived at their first destination. It could just be that one bag of coins from the place of striking – whether Rome or London – went to Bath, and a newly-healed devotee tipped the lot into the Spring as an enthusiastic thank offering. From Sulis-Minerva's point of view this was a bargain, because if he had gone to the money changer to buy gold and silver for her, she would have missed what the money changer took as his cut.

Then Walker compared the coins from Bath with the same sort from the mass of coins from Coventina's Well on Hadrian's Wall. The same dies were repeated and only a few new ones were added to the list: the coins on Hadrian's Wall were virtually the same batch as those 300 miles further south at Bath. This strongly suggests that, unless some very strange process of Religious Supply was in operation, the die-links were caused by the fact that an issue had been circulated in Britain and had stayed there. The matter of Rome or London was no further forward.

The next step was to notice that there were other issues which turned up in unusually large numbers at Bath, such as 54 examples of the dupondius of Marcus Aurelius as assistant (Caesar) to Antoninus Pius, with the reverse simply stating TRP VIIII (in the ninth year of his Tribunician Power/joint reign), and a picture of Mars the god of war walking to the right. There was nothing at all British in any sense about these coins, except that a quick check on German publications suggested that they seemed to be missing over there. Just like the Britannia issue they were quite heavily die-linked. It was impossible to check on (for instance) France or Italy, because so few coin finds from there are published. While the case for striking Britannia asses in Britain seemed quite sensible there is really no reason at all to suggest that an issue saying TRP VIIII would suit the British mentality. It now began to look as if certain issues from the mint at Rome were bagged up and sent completely, or almost completely, to Britain. Again, there were similar issues in Coventina's Well, and these were from similar dies with a few new ones added. More British issues were identified, and the whole superb piece of work was published in the report on the excavations.

At this point it was clear that certain issues of coins in the second century were bagged up as they came out of the mint, and sent off in their entirety to Britain. These issues had now been identified, so their supply could be mapped out. Even if we can find out all the dies that were cut and used we cannot know for certain how many coins each pair of dies struck, but there are guesses. My favourite guess is based on the fact that one person, David Sellwood, exasperated by the discussion of the subject, cut himself some bronze dies, poured some silver blanks, and got striking. He managed about 8000 coins from one pair of dies before the punch die (the die held in pincers and banged with hammer), broke down and became unusable. The die embedded in the anvil looked as if it could go much further with the occasional bit of first aid. I like to believe that if one modern experimenter could get 8000 coins out of a first attempt, with virtually no prior knowledge, a master-craftsman at the mint in Rome could at least equal the record, and perhaps do a bit better. Yes, in Rome the die would have been iron, so prone to corrosion, and more brittle at times, but harder. Yes, the blanks we are discussing are copper or bronze, so harder, but they can be heated and so made easier to strike. Yes, some dies will have split on the tenth blow, but others will have worn well. But as a minimum figure for the coins produced by a pair of dies, based on one modern experiment with dissimilar materials and a lot of fantasy, 10,000 coins is a figure that I like to believe in as an average.

David Walker worked at a time when the commonly held belief centred on 30,000 coins per die, but he played safe and brought this down to 20,000. Of course the numbers were all conjured out of the air, but they give a start to the process of moving from error towards truth. He reckoned that since Coventina's Well has added so few dies beyond those found at Bath, the majority of dies had been seen. Calculations could be done to work out how many extra dies would be found if the sample were to be doubled yet again. Since adding the Coventina's Well coins to the Bath coins produced only a small number of new dies, to add on two more similar samples would add even fewer, and eventually the additions would cease.

With issues identified, the dies counted and estimated, and a number plucked out of the air to be struck by each die, he was brave enough to give a figure for the actual supply of copper coinage to Britain in certain years. Did he think his numbers should be taken as a firm guide? 'It cannot be emphasised too strongly that these figures are very approximate' – his own words in the final report. Was he thanked and encouraged? Some hopes. Has his work been made the basis for all sorts of new ideas and extravaganzas as his detractors feared? They need not have worried. This is the background to the suggestion that the money available per head of the population in Britain around 150 was 2 sestertii, or its equivalent in smaller coin. Earlier in this chapter I changed that to a range from 0-30, which I think is a fair range of possible error.

44 *After the problems of the coinage in the third century, the basic coin was made in a very poor silvered bronze until 357. This coin of Constantine I (struck about 320) has a silvery sheen, but not much more*

I have missed out a further speculative stage in which Walker moved from his British issues to the other issues which make up the bulk of site-finds – it is perhaps worth filling in the gap. If a sample of site-finds is taken, including Bath or Coventina's Well or not as you prefer, then the 32 coins of the British issues in the sample are the remains from an estimated total which was once supplied. There might even be a rough standard whereby 10,000 coins supplied yield one loss in our sample. There is no reason to think that the British coins were lost more enthusiastically or meanly than any other coins, so this standard can be extended to suggest what circulation pool our current finds represent. Horrible, speculative, nasty, dangerous – but highly interesting and very exciting.

This was a first stab at solving a problem by a highly original thinker. The point at issue is not whether he got it right: even his actual answer is almost irrelevant. What matters is that he tried to think it out, put down his reasoning to ensure that anyone could follow what he did and correct it, or avoid pitfalls when they were pointed out, so that progress could be made and we could understand better what coins in Roman Britain were all about.

When he started work on his thesis Andrew Hobley was able to discuss the ideas generated from Bath with David Walker. He went on from there to look at the general idea of supplies of certain types of coin to certain areas within the empire, and came up with a number of conclusions. We could start at Bath and Coventina's Well, large deposits given to Sulis-Minerva and Coventina. Are those deposits typical of coins used and lost throughout Britain? While the records of the Well and the Bath coins are now easily to hand, it took a lot of work to gather together details of comparable material from many excavation reports all round the country. For Hadrian there was a total of 426 coins for Britain, 293 for Bath and 294 for Coventina. Amongst these totals the Britannia asses give Britain 22, Bath 39 and Coventina 3. The Coventina coins have probably been sorted out of the heap as specially desirable, but this leaves Bath with too many Hadrian Britannias for its total compared with general British finds. The same is true for Antoninus Pius's Britannia issue. The British sample has more sestertii, the religious deposits have more dupondii and asses. This makes reasonable, if slightly mean, sense in that you put the coins in your pocket in the collection plate rather than the notes from your wallet.

When Hobley journeyed over to mainland Europe one of his first discoveries was that the British issues identified by Walker were in general correct. While there were 85 Britannia asses in a general survey of site-finds in Britain, not including the water deposits, there was one from an archaeological context in Germany, two in large museum coin collections in Gaul, and two in the same sort of collections in Italy. This imbalance itself is interesting, but when open coin collections are removed it becomes an almost exact fit – provided of course we remember to check with other general issues to see that they really do spread throughout the provinces, and that the Britannia event is something unusual. One glance at Hobley's tables confirms the general circulation of coinage. As a random example we could take the sestertius of Antoninus Pius showing the standing figure of Aequitas (Fair shares, Equity?). 48 examples were found: Britain 2, NE Gaul 4, Lower (N) Germany 5, Upper (S) Germany 5, Raetia (roughly Switzerland) 2, Pannonia (roughly W Hungary) 2, Gaul 15, Italy 13.

Examples of particular coin types confined to particular provinces are rare; it is much more common to find a specific type which is spread over only two or three provinces, such as Upper and Lower Germany. There are very many examples of coins which are common on the mainland, but unknown here in the offshore island.

The results from these excellent pieces of work show not only that copper and bronze coins were distributed unequally throughout the western provinces, but even more clearly, that they moved very little once they had been supplied and sent into open circulation. The few that did travel, the exceptions, prove the rule.

An interlude

Before we reach the later empire there is a short period when all the previous rules break down; this is the time of the British Empire, the rule from Britain of the emperors Carausius and then Allectus. The early system of coinage had broken down so that the denarius had gone, the gold piece survived, and the bronze sestertius and dupondius, the copper as and its subdivisions were all things of the past. With the gold piece there was only the silver-copper coin with a radiate crown. Instead of unreliable supply from the single western mint in Rome, money was home-produced in Britain. Considering the work which David Walker and Andrew Hobley had to do, I find it very surprising indeed that the British episode is so little studied in detail. Shiel and Casey have both studied the reigns and their place in the wider picture; they and others have looked at the coins and the messages struck on them; but no one has yet started a detailed study of the one period in Roman Britain when we produced coinage for ourselves and so, presumably, satisfied our needs.

Gold was well produced, though not many coins survive to allow any sort of estimate of original production. Good silver was minted for the first time in well over a century, though again the number of examples is very small, so the information about the size of issues that can be drawn from them is limited. But copper coins with a dash of silver are common, often well preserved, and there for the study. Unfortunately we can say little about how those radiate coins were used because their relations either upwards to gold and real silver, or downwards to copper, are unknown and probably unknowable. The coins cannot be worth less than their small silver content, but even at 2% silver for the earlier coins, and perhaps 4% for the later coins this would be about 50p

45 *The portrayal of women on Roman coins is sporadic, and a detailed study of when they appear and when they are absent is still needed. This coin was minted about 338 by the sons of Constantine I to commemorate Constantine's step-mother Theodora*

or £1. A coinage system with units of £600 and £1 hardly deserves the name. It could be that the silvery surface of the coins allowed the state to get away with issuing them as equivalent to the old denarii. It is just possible that the economy and the coinage system in Carausian Britain were so sophisticated that they circulated as token silver coins. If that was so, why were real silver coins introduced halfway through the reign and how were they used? Perhaps the system of 290 was a foretaste of Diocletian's new system of 294 – with gold, silver and radiates of about 5 denarii (£1.25), all that was missing was the large silver-copper follis or nummus and the small very rare 2 denarius piece.

There is a lot that could be said and speculated about Carausius and Allectus, but as this section is aiming to deal mainly with coin use, we ought to move on.

Late silver and gold

Chapter 1 explained that the official line on silver and gold coins after Diocletian's great reform of 294 was that they were an essential and useful part of the system; chapter 2 explained that for the man-in-the-field or the woman-in-the-market this was a polite fiction. If they were ever seen it was only on tax day when one official sold you the coin, another took it back in taxes, and the soldiers looked on to see that you did not run away with it. But by the early fourth century you could probably circumvent the whole process and pay your taxes in kind.

So late silver and gold in Britain live and move briefly but strongly. The change seems to happen about 356, and after that there is the solidus, which perhaps due to its lower weight we ought to bring down to £500, heavy silver at perhaps £33 and light silver at £16. On this scale the Hoxne hoard of 565 gold coins and 14,000 silver comes out at £282,500 plus £224,000 – about half a million, not counting all the gold and silver objects. It sounds remarkable, but remember that it would not buy you a nice Jacobethan, triple-garaged house in the stockbroker belt, so what price a 50-roomed villa? Perhaps every Hoxne deserves a 50-roomed villa, and every 50-roomed villa involves a Hoxne, but the odd thing is the way that the desirable residences are mostly in the Cotswolds, and certainly not in East Anglia, whereas the purchase prices are in East Anglia, and there are none in the Cotswolds.

Gold, as always, was too valuable to lose, but as our quick survey of site-finds showed silver is actually lost, at the rate of about one late silver coin to 1000 copper coins. This means it was involved in the business of emendi et vendendi utilitas (buying and selling), as the Anonymus said it was.

Late copper

Just as the period 294 to the middle of the fourth century was a hazy time for precious metal coinage, so the small addition of silver to copper makes all speculation pointless. We do not know where we stand with the large coins of 294-306, the smaller coins of 306-13, the raised silver content after 313, the lowered silver content after 317, and so on. By 330 things were settling down, and the commonly produced coin has so little silver that we may be justified in setting it aside. Certainly site-finds, which increase dramatically after 330, suggest that the coinage was suddenly regarded with far less awe and care.

To avoid constant muddle and doubt I shall assume that the common copper coin of the fourth century varied around a value of five nummi: sometimes it was higher, sometimes a bit lower. The reason I do this is because when the Vandals in Carthage made their own copper coins for the first time they looked, weighed, and felt very like the common copper coins of the eastern empire, but had on the reverse IIII, which is taken to mean four nummi. Apart from reasons of simplicity there is an ulterior motive which has already been mentioned; in the later fifth century when you wanted to change a gold solidus you received 7000 nummi; when you needed to buy one, you had to pay 7200 nummi. This links the nummus, whatever that was, to the gold piece. And if we give our common copper coins of the fourth century the value of five nummi, that gives 1400 to the gold piece. In turn this suggests a modern value for the copper coin of around 30-40p. Since there were always old and scrappy coins around which could have been given a general notional value such as 5p, a market-stall-type economy could have worked with the coins we find on site today.

If all the worrying suggestions, calculations, extrapolations, and sheer inventions cancel out then we might be able to see something in the long term. The short-term changes are of course the subject of stuffy scholarship and the life-blood of the academic, but they are all more or less speculative and probably get near to nullifying one another. But there is a change between around AD 100, when the coin system of Britain was more or less settling down, and AD 400, when it was in terminal bloom. Forgetting modern values because they are both distracting and introduce likely errors, it is quite clear that the average value of coins found of the reign of Trajan was around the sestertius, or 1/100 of the heavier gold piece while the average coin of the time around 400 was the small copper, or 1/1400 of the smaller gold piece. That might mean that 300 years of 'having an economy' had persuaded the Britons that little discs of copper were quite useful for simplifying the exchange of goods. What a pity they had to wait for over 1200 years for those useful discs of copper to come back.

6 Britain and abroad

The use of coinage arrived in Britain somewhere in the last few centuries BC, and left sometime in the early fifth century AD. There may have been a few odd coins which appeared in Britain in, say, the fourth century BC, and there certainly were a few coins which turned up in the fifth century AD, but I am talking about the idea of the general use of coinage. One swallow does not make a summer; and neither does one Greek tetradrachm nor one Gothic solidus a coin-using community make.

In the period of the use of Roman coins, just under 400 years, there were only 40 years in which Britain housed an official mint; therefore it was totally dependent on mainland Europe for the support of this foreign fashion. The mint in Britain is difficult to describe without elaboration. I have just described it as 'official', but as it started under the rebel emperor Carausius, the shade of the official emperor, Diocletian, would not approve. The mint seems to be plural at that point, for there are two quite different common mint-marks, and several others as well. LON is fairly clearly London, but C or G, CL or GL, is strongly disputed: Colchester is a common favourite, although I favour Glevum (Gloucester). All this can be followed up in the works devoted to the episode of Carausius and Allectus. Gold, silver and copper-silver was produced, so it is fair to say that Britain satisfied its own need for coins: certainly no one else was likely to. This accounts for the 10 years from 286-96.

After that, from 296-*c*.326, the mint of London formed a fully-operational part of Diocletian's newly organised Imperial Mint of Rome (provincial branches) Plc. The issues from London followed faithfully the empire-wide pattern, so that the only difference from products of Alexandria or Thessalonica lay in the mint-mark which always included L, and often LN or LON. There were occasional divergences; for instance the first issues from London are highly untypical in having no mint mark. Since everywhere else does identify its issues then London products are quite clear, but why the absence? One suggestion was that the mint was a re-organised rebel mint which should not speak its name, for a few years at least, until the fuss had died down.

It is just possible that this could gain credibility by a further leap of fantasy. Under Carausius there had been the impolite fiction that Britain was a full part of the empire, and that Carausius was just one of the several emperors charged with ruling different parts of that sprawling state. This fiction was broadcast by Carausius, and on his coins. A common reverse type, especially in times of struggle and danger, was Pax Aug, Pax Augusti, the peace of (created by, caused by, guarded by) the Augustus or emperor. If there were two emperors it became Pax Augustorum, of the plural emperors, and this was abbreviated to Augg. Three emperors, and the legend became Pax Auggg.

The two official Augusti, Diocletian and his colleague Maximian, struck coins to celebrate their peacefulness with reverses of Pax Augg. But there were other coins in circulation which seemed just the same in shape and weight and silveryness, and one had three portraits on – Diocletian, Maximian and, in the third place, Carausius. The obverse proclaimed Carausius et Fratres Sui, Carausius and his brothers as emperors, and the reverse did roughly the same by noting the peace of the three Augusti, Pax Auggg. This could be laughed off as Carausius having a go at self-proclamation. It was more difficult to dismiss coins of perfect standard, excellently produced, with exact portraits and titles of Diocletian or Maximian, but with a clear message, Pax Auggg. These seemed to show that the official, or central emperors agreed that there were three emperors – until you looked at the mint-mark, which was invariably the Lon or C/G mint from Britain. Legitimate use of all possible resources; disgraceful misuse of the sacred mint. The contempt should be purged by several years in limbo.

The other deviation of the London mint was to strike only the large copper-silver coins, the folles or nummi, perhaps of 25 denarii by 301. Not trusting the former rebel mint with gold or silver is fairly understandable, and perhaps quite a wise precaution. The absence of the radiate coin, perhaps of 5 denarii, is more difficult to understand, but these were not struck outside the Mediterranean area. The nearest mint to Britain to strike these was Pavia (Ticinum). If everything I have said about higher values and prices in the Mediterranean area, and lower prices in the provinces is even half correct, then the failure to mint the smallest coin, possibly two denarii, is strange. This is just the coin that Britain might well have needed, and it is just the coin that it never received – in line with most of the rest of the empire. It is as if there was policy and production, two different ideas, in two different ministries, and they were kept firmly apart. Yes, of course the new coinage system caters for all sorts and conditions of people, from the highest to the lowest. All wants are filled – in theory. Back at the mint, we do what we always have, none of your new fangled social theory. We have always struck one main coin from time immemorial, well since my grandfather, and we are going on in the old way.

This division between base metal coinage and silver and gold makes the point yet again that although the face values come quite close to one another – the follis was probably one quarter of the silver piece, and it contained up to 3 or 4% silver – the two categories were seen as very different. Britain was probably fit to produce base metal coinage for the masses; or those parts of the masses who used coins; well, those parts of the masses to whom a five pound note was a basic everyday affair, but who were not fit to dabble in sacred areas of gold and silver. Yet in the late fourth century we know there was a treasury, probably concerned with gold and silver, at London. And in around 383 another usurper, Magnus Maximus, struck an issue of gold coins of excellent standard, probably in London, before he set off to seize the whole empire. Perhaps this is the crux of the matter: Britain is too separate a place to have a means of sacred self-proclamation – silver and gold coinage, which makes it quite clear that the man on the obverse has arrived. He strikes the coinage, the army demand gold and silver coinage, the army is his – for the time being.

From 296-*c*.326 the mint at London struck standard Roman coinage which moved out into the surrounding provinces, and even turns up in the eastern Mediterranean in small amounts. In the same way, coins produced in non-British mints came into Britain. Perhaps that ought to be 'at the same time', though even that causes doubts. We do not know how the coins moved, but perhaps it is safe to assume that they only moved when they formed a full part of the coin-using pool. For the period when Britain had its own mint, it should be safe to say that non-British coins arrived by something approaching accident (this clearly applies only to copper, because gold and silver had to be sent in from outside). I have a touching faith in reason, even in the Roman administration, and I am loath to believe that the mint-master at Trier or Lyon or Arles bagged up a consignment of his copper coins to be sent to Britain; and if he did it by accident once or twice, it seems unlikely that it was a regular thing.

So how did the copper coins minted at Trier, Lyon and Arles, and even further afield, arrive in Britain? The answer 'in trade' seems to me unsatisfactory the moment you begin to unpick it. It is most unlikely that consignments of goods from London to Lyon were paid for by sending back the equivalent amount of small change; if money changed hands then it was probably gold. This was forbidden in the 370s, but extreme doubts have been expressed as to whether the prohibition worked. However, the idea of using coin to pay for goods at a long distance has two major problems: firstly, it is based on the assumption that the deal went through between a person based in London and another in Lyon, and that the goods were then despatched by carrier or parcel post; and secondly, even if the London trader took the goods to Lyon, or got one of his workers to do it, why come back with just a bag of gold? Why not use whatever transport had been used on the way out to bring back something in exchange which could be profitably sold in London? It is even more likely that the process had several stages and a number of middlemen. When all these factors have been taken into account, I prefer the explanation for the movement of coin as 'with traders and others' rather than 'in trade'. Everyone who came into the province carried with them small change, which was uniform over the whole empire (I look forward eagerly to the day when this state returns, if only just for Europe as a start). When they were here, incomers used money, and their Gallic or German money box contents became more British. They returned home, and the contents of their money boxes lost their Britishness and returned to being Gallic.

46 *Religion as shown on coins under Constantine I, who supported Christianity, could usually be interpreted according to the preference of the observer. On this coin, struck after Constantine's death, a Christian might see Constantine ascending to heaven in a fiery chariot, like an old testament prophet. A pagan would see a perfectly satisfactory apotheosis in which the emperor, at death, became a god*

There is scope for a lot of future work here, but for the moment I can simply quote the coins of Constantine's son Crispus, who appears from 317-26. This is within the period of the London mint, yet not all of his coins in Britain are from London. At Cirencester there were 36, of which London provides 12, Lyon 2 and Trier 22. This can be checked at Verulamium where there were 30 coins: London 9, Lyon 4, Trier 11, Ticinum (Pavia) 2, Rome 1, Aquileia 1 and Siscia 2. London coins of this period (296-326) occur very widely, but always in fairly small numbers – pulling books off the shelf almost at random found them at Sardis in Asia Minor, Luxembourg, Zilil in Morocco, and Conimbriga in Portugal. If the Cirencester and Verulamium figures are supported elsewhere in Britain, it looks as if home-grown coins were in a minority.

I could of course have followed my own advice and looked at a group of concentrated coin finds of a particular period (i.e. a hoard), instead of getting irritated chasing small numbers of coins through a large number of different sources. But the problem here is always the question of where the hoard was gathered together. The fact that the hoard was found in Britain does not mean that the coins were extracted from circulation there. But surely it will be obvious? If there are a lot of London coins it is a hoard of British coins; if not, then it was formed somewhere else. The numbers for coins of Crispus at Cirencester and Verulamium ought to dispose of a circular argument like that. If I had given just the numbers and not the locations then Cirencester would be somewhere in the north-east of France perhaps – nearer Trier than London, and Verulamium ought to be further south, but perhaps still in France.

The episode of 286-326 divides the remaining years of Roman coin use in Britain neatly into two. It actually sits on the dividing line between the Rome mint domination of the early empire, and the widespread mint system of the later empire.

Abroad

In order to compare Britain with the rest of the Roman world, we have to find out what there is abroad. This, at present, is a very unsatisfactory state of affairs, as a brief outline will show.

In Germany all is almost well. True to the British caricature of the Germans, a massive survey was started in the 1950s in which every Roman coin found in (West) Germany was to be published. Known as FMRD (Fundmünzen der römischen Zeit in Deutschland - Coin finds of the Roman period in Germany), this survey has advanced so that large areas of the countryside, inside and outside the empire, have been examined parish by parish. This means that when we want to know if a certain coin has been found in Germany there is a good chance of finding out. It takes time to look through, parish by parish, but you soon get to know the sites which have hundreds of coins, and flick quickly through the many small villages which have one or two Roman coins to their name.

There are problems for the high-speed searcher. The point at which I most often get tangled up is the running serial number for all the coins from a site. Only where absolutely everything is the same – denomination, emperor, issue date, mint, reverse, as well as find spot and present location, or published reference – does a single line of text cover more than one coin. This trips me up time and again, because I run down the page counting the lines of the coins in which I am interested and then find that two lines had not a single running serial number but two, 44-56. So for instance if I had got to 15 coins, how many are there between 44 and 56, 12 or 13? I have to stop and think, lose my total and start all over again. The references depend on the time when the coins were first published. If this was before Roman Imperial coinage was started in 1923, the references tend to be to the old and faulty volumes of Cohen. But which libraries still hold copies of Cohen, and how many individuals have a set? And why is there not a concordance – at least available on line – to transfer Cohen numbers into proper modern references? But my German and Fundmünzen friends will be getting annoyed at this quibbling, because they know very well that compared with many other places in Europe, their house is in immaculate order.

Luxembourg have followed the same route of a Fundmünzen, as have Slovenia, Hungary and Austria, with the result that if you have access to a good library you have access to coins from those countries. Italy quite rightly has its own abbreviation RMR, Ritrovamenti monetali di eta Romana nel Veneto (Coin finds of the Roman period in the area of the Veneto). The title warns that the project started in the north-east of Italy, with the nerve centre in the University of Padua, but I understand that it is now to be extended so that it will eventually cover the whole of the country.

All these series cover single finds, site-finds and hoards. France has a series devoted to coin hoards of the Roman period, and the same criticisms apply to that as to the Robertson volume for Britain. In the early period they are all very useful, but in the fourth century there is trouble. Spain, so far, does not have any such series.

You may wonder where all the great Roman sites of the Mediterranean have got to; Ephesus, Priene, Constantinople, Alexandria, Cyrene . . . the list could be added to easily from any guide book or travel brochure. The simple answer is that apart from honourable exceptions, the great cities are disaster areas. They have been plundered for years by foreign diggers in the name of archaeology, yet in only a very few cases have any coins been examined or published. In a few cases it is said that the coins were given away or distributed as they came up.

The exceptions which are quoted again and again are Antioch and Sardis (Turkey), Athens and Corinth (Greece), and Histria (Romania). There are smaller groups from many places such as Constantinople, Troy and especially Jerusalem, but when the coins are to be split up into 21 periods, or more, then a sample of less than about 200 is of limited use. Publications continue for Carthage, and are in the pipeline for Cyrene, Aphrodisias, and for several different excavations in Jerusalem. Returning to the west end of the Mediterranean there are very useful reports for Zilil in Morocco, and Clunia and Belo in Spain, and a magnificent volume for Conimbriga in Portugal.

That is the positive side; the negative side is almost every other site you have ever heard of, allowing for the ones I always forget, and the few where publication has taken place, but I have never seen it or heard of it.

The early Empire

We still have to find actual coins that came into Britain before the army of AD 43. If John Creighton's ideas on top British families sending sons to Rome, either to get a bit of polish, or as polite hostages, is correct, then some Republican and Augustan denarii must have come back from Rome when they returned. Traders, who are suspected at certain sites in the home counties, are unlikely to have shed all their Roman money as they crossed the Channel. But so far, no coin struck before AD 43 has turned up in an undoubted archaeological context of the same date.

This means that if we stick to the material as it survives we have to begin with the coins brought with them by the armies. Most of the details have been given in the early chapters on what Rome produced and what got to Britain, so there is no need for repetition. What needs discussion and investigation is the make-up of the early coinage used and lost: the proportion of the different denominations and metals found, in comparison to the mainland. The only detailed work that I know on this was done some years ago by Ian Hodder on material that I had collected in Britain, France and Italy. The problem with that material is that most of it came from museum collections, it is now over 30 years out of date, and it needs to be replaced by real coins from excavations.

The general picture that resulted from Hodder's mapping showed a concentration of higher value coins in the Mediterranean area before about AD 50, and then a gradual spread of higher denominations such as the sestertius up through the Rhone/Rhine corridor to reach Britain later in the second century. This makes good sense as a demonstration of the gradual rise in coin use and prices in Britain to reach the Mediterranean levels just as the early coinage system based on the as and the denarius died out. Inflation can be seen expanding out from Italy and creeping up the map to reach Britain in due course. This picture is probably supported by the few groups of excavated coins that we have, but since the bulk of the material comes from museum collections it is open to another, less exciting, explanation.

The higher value coins are either the larger bronze or the silver coins. These are more attractive and sought after than the duller asses and dupondii; any collector would prefer to show off his collection of well-preserved sestertii than a mixture of worn coins of all shapes, sizes, and dates. From the workmen employed in digging the sewer trenches and planting vines the discriminating collector will take the best, and leave the worse. The workman in turn will learn which coins fetch the best prices and the warmest smiles and will select for himself. So the 'good' nineteenth-century collection will have been selected for modern appeal, which coincides with ancient value. Most big museum collections on the mainland derive from a small number of nineteenth-century worthies and collectors, so they, in turn, may well be biased against the little coin. This might be worst in Italy, the French may be more archaeologically minded, and the British may save everything – being a nation of small shopkeepers. This would give exactly the same type of maps as those that Hodder produced.

I don't think the second story is the right one, because although some museum collections are obviously too 'good', that can only be seen in relation to less discriminating collections; and some museums when I visited them were the depots of local archaeological groups, and the coins they had found were set out in cases still with their covering of mud. These museum collections correspond very well with groups of coins known to have been found in excavations. The rule must always be to start from the archaeological groups, to compare these with museum collections, and to use museum collections where they show general similarities to known site-finds. Working in this way, the problem I have outlined can be shown to be a fairly limited one. It applies as much to British museums as to mainland ones.

To summarise: in the AD 40s Britain had to be provided with a full suite of coins. This was quite different from the position on the continent, where coin supply had been operating for half a century or more. In turn this meant that what was in circulation was only that which was supplied or home-produced when supply failed; there was no circulation pool from the past to act as a cushion in times of coin shortage. The reason for supplying Britain was to pay soldiers and other state servants, so the basis was silver and gold; and enough bronze was supplied, when it was produced by the mint, to oil the wheels of change and circulation. By the end of the reign of Nero most denominations were getting to Britain, but research in the future may find that there is more medium denominations, dupondii and asses, than large (sestertii) or small (semisses and quadrantes) change present than in, say, Italy. Use of all denominations continued through the second century, but supply of sestertii for some reason stopped around 200, and those already in Britain were continuously used almost to extinction.

For the majority of the period of radiate coins Britain was part of the Gallic empire, centred in Cologne. Britain was also part of the Barbarous Radiate confederation – whatever that was. The mapping of Barbarous Radiates has not yet been done in any detail, but there does seem to be an area where they predominate, and that is Europe north of the river Loire (which of course includes Britain). Kevin Butcher has just told me of examples soon to be published from Beirut, and pointed out that there are two copies of Tetricus at Sardis, and a group of over 20 just called Barbarous Radiates. The presence of large numbers of Barbarous Radiates at any site gives a bulge of coins at a time when coin loss is usually quite normal. This immediately marks out sites as being in the Barbarous Radiate realm.

The later Empire

The period from 296-326 when Britain had a mint of its own in London has been covered, while the drift of coins from other mints into Britain at that time has been noted but as yet cannot be accounted for in any detail. Coins from other mints came to Britain, coins from the London mint ventured out over most of the empire, but in smaller numbers as the distance increased. Coins in Rome follow the same pattern as coins in Britain – in a way. Rome minted its own coins throughout the fourth century, and presumably no mint-master outside Rome would have dared to bag up some of his products and send them to help supply the Eternal City with coin. Yet when Rome and Other coins are compared, there is fluctuation throughout the century; sometimes Rome coins are in a majority, while at other times (such as 364-78), Rome coins are submerged by many coins from outside. And just as London coins turn up in

Rome, so Rome coins turn up in Britain. The Other coins must, I think, be the result of troop movements, traders, travellers, and other unspecified drift, and this supports the picture I drew for Britain.

In the period between 326-402 the mints of Trier, Lyon and Arles struck most of the coins which appear in Britain, and this is also true for all the north-western provinces. Deep in south Germany there is influence from both the Balkan mints coming up through Austria, and the eastern mints, probably coming up the Danube from the Black Sea. In the south of France the Italian mints, Rome and Aquileia, provided a number of coins. But there is a large area in which the three mints predominate. The question I always want to ask when I get on to this subject is 'What is the pattern?' Perhaps part of this compulsion is the apparent total absence of pattern in Britain. Every site seems to have roughly the same proportions of the three mints for each period of issue. In 330-48 Trier predominates heavily; from 364-78 Lyon and Arles provide the majority of coins. The mix of mints is so uniform that I once suggested in sheer exasperation that there was a depot somewhere in the north of France where coin was received for despatch to Britain, but was always very thoroughly stirred before despatch.

That is certainly nonsense, but two points which need to be investigated grow out of it. Is there an area in the north of France where the balance of mints is roughly the same as it is in Britain? If so, what does this say about the relationship of Britain to the mainland at that time? Secondly, how can the uniform British mix be accounted for if the Coin Stirrer did not exist? The first question cannot be answered as yet, because we just do not have enough published evidence on mint distributions at sites in the north of France.

The matter of uniformity in Britain compared with the mainland cannot be explained, but there might be room for speculation. All coin struck after 326, except for copies, had to be imported into Britain. In a less ridiculous form, the Coin Stirrer theory suggests that coin was imported into Britain already mixed. How this happened in 364-78, when Lyon and Arles were the main producers, I cannot yet imagine. Obviously the minor constituents such as Rome and Aquileia can be accounted for by trade drift; but it is extremely unlikely that the mints of Lyon and Arles sent their British quotas to a mixing point and that the coins were supplied from there to Britain. The alternative must be true: that Lyon and Arles supplied their products direct to Britain. Why then are there not pockets of Lyon coins and pockets of Arles coins as different bags were sent to different places, or even landed at different places?

Did all incoming coin go through London? How did it travel on from there? Supply from London to York and the North is far better done by sea than by land; it is safer, quicker, and when heavy weights are involved, much easier. Since no patterns have yet been even suspected the answer seems to be that the mixing was done in Britain by the simple process of using the coins. We ought really to expect this after the Barbarous Radiate episode, an era where there are direct links between coins found in Belgium, the middle of

France, the south coast of Britain and points further north. These unofficial coins, produced in so many different styles, and presumably in a number of places, must have been fed into a remarkably active coin circulation to produce the distributions and lack of local patterning visible today. In the same way we probably have to assume that discrete bags of coin arrived in Britain from Lyon and Arles, were let out into circulation at different places, and that for a short time after there were indeed concentrations of Lyon coins around a given town or fort. However, it seems that coin use was so active that such patterns were destroyed within a short time by the quick movement of coin about the provinces.

The oddity of Britain in the fourth century compared with other places is that there are a lot of both copies and coins in general about. As always, this applies to copper coin – gold and silver remain rare as losses everywhere. It is possible that the two points are connected, but we are not yet in a position to find out. It could be that the majority of the bulge of British coins is due to the copies; that official coins are uniformly distributed, used, lost and found over the north-west empire, but copies in Britain make it look as if there were more coins in use there. In the period 364-78 this is almost certainly not true, because although there seem to be few copies, Britain shows a bulge. In the period 330-48 Britain has many copies, and this could account for our bulge in that era, but we do not yet know how many of those common coins are copies. At that period, as I mentioned earlier, there is a smooth transition from obviously a copy to obviously an official coin, with a majority of coins coming at the transition point. Mike Hammerson wrote a thesis on this question some years ago, and as a result, those who heard about it or read it suddenly found far more copies of coins than they had before. If more work is done and published there is a strong likelihood that the balance will change yet again.

The end of coinage in Britain is the same as the end of coinage in all areas away from the Mediterranean area. It is not that Britain comes adrift from Europe, but that the north-west provinces were no longer supplied with coin after *c*.400. The state, as usual, worried mainly about gold and silver because that is what the recipients worried about. The gold and silver supply stopped, so further supply of copper, or even the home-producing of copies, became irrelevant.

Britain went into the same non-coin-using phase as Gaul and Germany, without the Gothic copies of Roman gold probably produced in southern Gaul; and different regions emerged back into coin-using as the Germanic kingdoms got themselves organised. The 38 gold coins in the great ship burial at Sutton Hoo all come from different small mints in the Merovingian empire, mainly towns in modern France, and may have been deposited somewhere around 620-30. Not long after that the first Anglo-Saxon gold coinage began, following the mainland pattern, and from there the use of precious metal coinage in Britain was continuous up to 1948.

Appendices

1 Archaeology

Working with Roman coins in Britain is mainly connected, for me, with the coins that archaeologists have dug up in the course of their excavations or gathered in the course of survey and field-walking. The only hoards I have even got my hands on have been the scruffy type of the late third and late fourth centuries which turn up quite often in rubbish levels on excavations. The coins range from 3-20, perhaps half are just legible, and no self-respecting collector would give any of them a second glance. Turning years of experience of working on site-finds into a book on the various aspects of Roman coinage in Britain means distilling archaeological material into narrative. Since most people have not had the benefit of working on an excavation, and even less have seen what goes in to turning the records and observations up into a published report, the archaeological details from which the ideas come have had to be relegated to this appendix.

The main connection to the earlier chapters comes in chapter 2 where I outlined the relationship between what coins were struck in the official mints, which categories came to Britain, and what Britain produced unofficially for itself. I went on from there to suggest what this meant in terms of circulation of coin, the lifespan of the different issues and categories, and therefore the likely date at which a group of coins might be lost. An example could be the period after 274 when Aurelian reformed the very low standard radiate coinage, and 294 when Diocletian instituted even more reforms. All this high standard coinage lasted from *c.*274-*c.*330; meanwhile the old radiate coins of low value, and the Barbarous Radiates of very low value, supplied the need for small change.

So far, so good; the story makes sense, and ideas for dating are fairly obvious. If high-value coinage was new coinage, then market stall transactions took place with the help of old, low-value coinage. To say that a Barbarous Radiate was probably struck between 270-86 when Carausius produced coin in and for Britain is to talk about the date of striking and not the date of use or, even less, the date of loss. The next common coin is likely to be an issue of 330-5, and old small change will probably be needed up to that date. The date of use of Barbarous Radiates may well stretch from 270-330. If a mosaic pavement is lifted, and the layer underneath is dug, and two Barbarous Radiates are found, what is the likely date at which the pavement was laid?

First it cannot have been laid before 260 when the coins that some Barbarous Radiates copy were struck. Second, the wave of Barbarity probably got going strongly after about 274, so the pavement is probably later than that. There are no coins of Carausius so the pavement may be before 296. As Barbarous Radiates are probably needed until about 320-30, the pavement may be as late as 330. Notice the gradation: must be later than 260, probably later than 274, may be before 296, may be as late as 330.

Supposing there were 10 coins, and they consisted of various radiates, official and barbarous, but no Carausius or Allectus, and no later coins; tell us the chances that the pavement is before 296 or after 320. Give us a set of tables of the way that groups of coins hang together, tell us the numbers to expect. Tell us the number of radiates that make it quite clear that the coin of 330-5 is really missing because it had not yet been minted, rather than missing by chance because the group is not big enough to expect it.

Such requests, sometimes demands, have followed every occasion time I have talked or written about the problem. What followed every time are the statements that at present I cannot do it, that in future someone else might be able to do it, and that the publishing of coin finds has to change.

At present I can give an impression – if it had been deposited after 330 I would have expected at least one coin of 330-5 in that group of 10 coins. The response may be that my impression is not good enough; we want facts. The facts would consist of lists of groups of coins from archaeological deposits with their place in the stratigraphy of the site and therefore their likely date of deposition. All I have to do is go through excavation reports and collect the information. Since it is obviously so basic and so useful, why has this not been done?

This problem was discussed at a meeting in 1973 and as a result John Collis added to the publication which resulted, *Coins and the Archaeologist*, a short article on 'Data for Dating', on just this subject. He included a pull-out sheet for excavators to note down the coins that had occurred together in layers or phases which they could send back to him, and he would do all the work of collecting, collating, and publishing. He got not one reply. The only excavator who actually thought of doing it, so far as I know, was the excavator ofVerulamium, Sheppard Frere, but even he was daunted by the work it would involve. He has an excuse because of the size of his site; but excavators of smaller sites cannot be let off so lightly.

The general reader, not familiar with excavation reports, who has braved this appendix is likely to ask with incredulity 'You mean people dig things, write reports, but then don't publish what they found where? So what do they publish?' The answer of course is whatever they consider to be relevant to the site they are publishing; they do not always consider that some of their information might be used in the future for purposes above and beyond the site in hand. To be fair, and it is quite an effort, no one can know at a given moment what information may be wanted by some bright young research student in the future, and you cannot publish every grain of soil. On the other hand this fairly strong want was published nearly 30 years ago, and people are still not responding even though it is crystal clear that the information is wanted.

The thing that holds people back is concentrating on their site and not looking outside their own trenches. They have a sequence of layers, floors and rubbish deposits one on top of the other, containing coins and pottery, and a rough idea of the dating – the lowest floor is first-century, the middle floor *c*.300, the top floor *c*.390. Between the middle and top floor, and therefore clearly in the fourth century between 300-90, there are several coins which run from Hadrian, through some radiates of about 250, to three coins of 330-48. For dating the sequence the only coins which matter are the three fourth-century coins because the others are clearly out of sequence, recycled rubbish, or heirlooms. They add nothing to dating the sequence and since they are out of place it is good enough to say that the coins in the layer were three coins of 330-48, and a few others of earlier date.

This is true enough for the single layer that they are considering, but if only they looked a little more widely they would find that there is quite a growth industry in saying things about sites from the total number of coins found, the presences and absences, and the numbers found at different dates compared with a regional average. This is beginning to sink in, so most people now mention the 'important' coins (those three of 330-48), and then give a total coin list among the reports on things found. This has taken time, energy, and some bad temper to bring about; but there are still organisations that up to now have only conserved the coins that will help in dating, and those from sealed Roman deposits, so full coin lists have not been on the agenda, and there are still sites under excavation where no coin lists are likely to be published. Only when the publication of all the coins excavated from a site becomes the norm can we hope for real progress; and only when those coins are published as stratigraphic groups can we move forward.

To return to the list that I ought to have prepared, which would give the contents of different excavated layers so that any excavator could compare his coins from layer 6 with summary charts and read off a likely date: the reason that the list has not been made is that it would include only about 10 sites – and I think I exaggerate – and their 1200 coins. This vital information has not been published, so we still rely on impressions. If only three excavators read this, take note and publish accordingly, I will think that the book has been worthwhile.

2 Numbers

As I explained in the introduction I promised myself that I would try to avoid all diagrams and talk of numbers in writing this book, except for this brief aside tucked well away in an appendix. Numbers almost came in when I was comparing the coins from Cirencester and Verulamium, but I nobly restrained myself and promised that those who wanted the full list could find them here. I therefore start out with a list of the Verulamium coins, period by period, and then reduce them to the equivalent number of coins per 1000. This pretends that if there were only 1000 coins in the Verulamium list, this is what they would have been. The same is done for Cirencester. In the final column comes the survey of 140 British sites of all possible sorts – villas, towns, temples, forts and villages. Again, it is expressed as coins per 1000.

Date	Verulamium		Cirencester		British Mean
	Number	per 1000	Number	per 1000	per 1000
to AD 41	63	7	66	7	6
41-54	98	11	135	14	12
54-69	74	8	59	6	6
69-96	218	24	279	28	31
96-117	127	14	120	12	20
117-38	119	13	98	10	16
138-61	125	14	139	14	19
161-80	74	8	92	9	12
180-93	30	3	32	3	5
193-222	86	9	137	14	15
222-38	44	5	73	7	7
238-60	58	6	105	11	8
260-75	2054	225	1076	108	144
275-96	1773	194	819	82	121
296-317	94	10	123	12	17
317-30	260	28	543	54	44
330-48	1906	209	2242	225	246
348-64	1162	127	1073	108	98
364-78	609	67	1320	132	118
378-88	11	1	82	8	5
388-402	156	17	1368	137	50
Total	9141		9981		

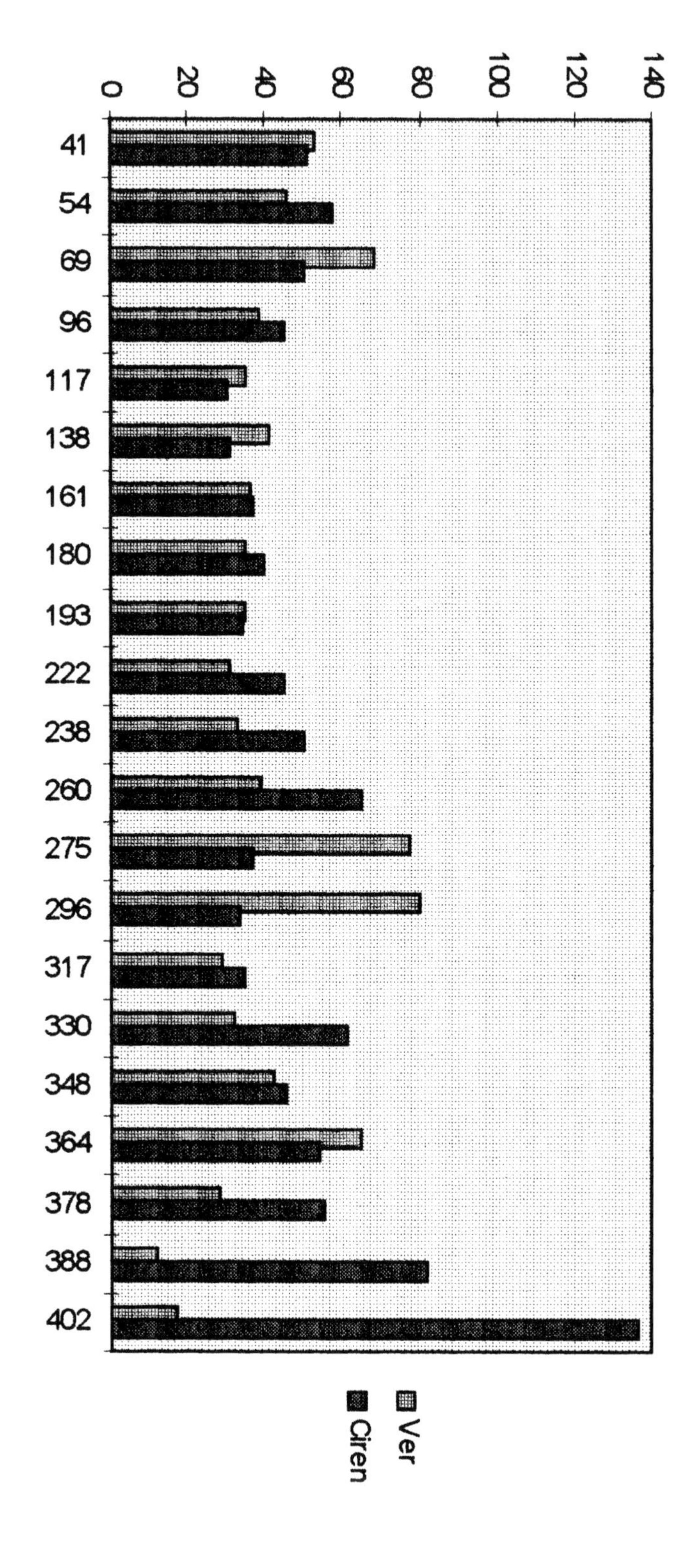

Fig. 1 *Verulamium and Cirencester compared with twice the mean*

When numbers are expressed in as simple and uncluttered form as those above, it seems a pointless complication to talk of further methods of dealing with them. A glance down the columns compares Verulamium with Cirencester, and the reduction to coins per 1000 is almost irrelevant when the two sites have such similar totals of coins. If we had to compare one site with 4923 coins with another with 11,067 then reduction to a proportion of 100 (percentages) or 1000, would be essential.

My problem is to keep in mind the comparison between Cirencester and the mean in one period while I look for the same comparison in another period. I much prefer to put the material on a diagram so that I can see all the points of similarity and difference at once, and at the same scale as in **fig. 1**. This, for me, puts all the words of the comparison attempted in chapter 4 into one exact, succinct diagram. All that is needed for interpretation is the understanding that since the towns' results are made a percentage of twice the British mean, a value of 50 will show the town equalling the mean, and a value of 100 will show the town reaching a value of twice the mean. In a well-ordered, or well-behaved gathering of results, the mean will lie roughly in the middle and the separate values will lie some above and some below. Since all the values are positive the mean will lie halfway up the scale from zero to the highest value (so twice the mean). Any value above that can be considered odd, way-out, badly-behaved, or however else you like to express it. The only value in our whole gathering which exceeds twice the mean is the last value for Cirencester (388-402), and this can already be seen to be way-out just in the table of numbers.

This is the best method I have found, after much experimenting, for comparing one or two sites against the British mean. It gets fogged up when there are more than one or two sites, and it would be very difficult to use to sort a large number of sites into groups with similar characteristics.

For that purpose I use a diagram which is not much more difficult either to construct or to understand. First the coins per 1000 for each town are added up. This inevitably starts at zero and ends at 1000. If the process went uniformly the result would be straight line, but the British habit is to add on far fewer coins in the early period, and far more coins in the later period. If this is plotted on a diagram the line therefore starts climbing slowly, accelerates violently in the period after 260 as we have found in several earlier chapters, and ends strongly. If the British mean is included in the diagram the picture looks like **fig. 2**.

This demonstrates the relationship between the two sites and the mean, but it brings all the values very close together. In this case with just two sites of different characteristics all is well because both sites are only a little below the mean up to 260, then Verulamium takes off more than Cirencester and the two separate out on either side of the mean. We can use far more of the space available if we look only at the difference between each site and the mean, and that is represented in **fig. 3**. In each case the mean value has been taken away

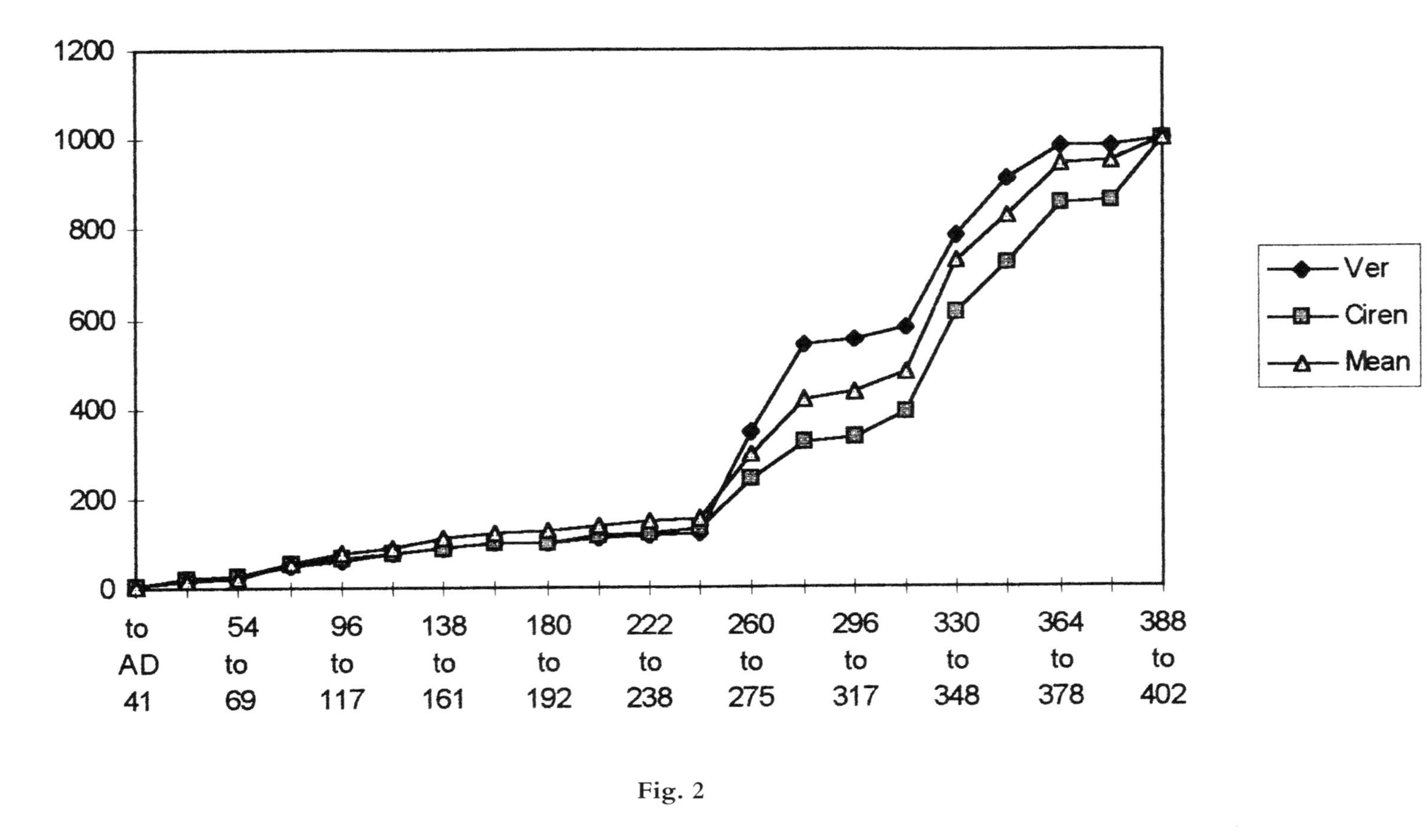
1200
1000
800
600
400
200
0
to AD 41
54 to 69
96 to 117
138 to 161
180 to 192
222 to 238
260 to 275
296 to 317
330 to 348
364 to 378
388 to 402
Ver
Ciren
Mean

Fig. 2

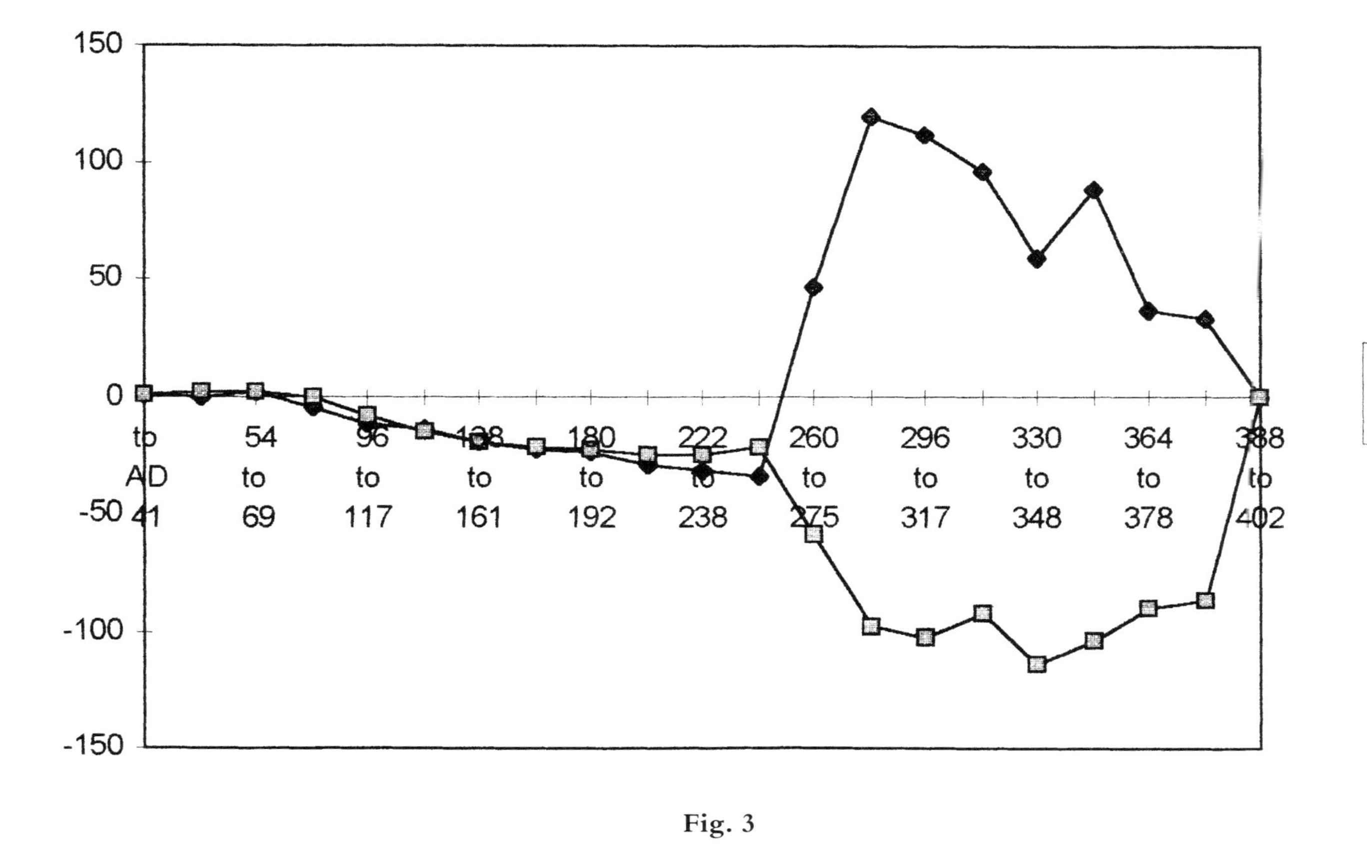
150
100
50
0
-50
-100
-150
to AD 41
54 to 69
96 to 117
138 to 161
180 to 192
222 to 238
260 to 275
296 to 317
330 to 348
364 to 378
388 to 402
Ver
Ciren

Fig. 3

from the town value, so the central zero line represents the mean. Verulamium moves sharply above the mean after 260, Cirencester does not keep up with the mean, falls below and moves downwards. After 296 Cirencester wobbles and then starts a steady upward movement – stronger than the mean. Verulamium fails to keep up with the mean after 275 and constantly adds on less coins than the mean, so moving downwards. In a diagrammatic sense this explains the British mean. Verulamium is characteristic of a good town site and the early military sites; Cirencester is characteristic of the bad towns, and many smaller settlements, villas and villages. The mean therefore lies in between.

This method is extremely useful for sorting out a collection of sites to see which are similar and which have their own peculiarities. Sorting out 100 sites is not too long a job; the diagrams can be printed out ten to a sheet, and each profile does not have to be compared with every other one to form groups because the Cirencester and the Verulamium move apart at a glance. The second printing can segregate the two major varieties and begin to cut the major categories into sub-sections. The trouble comes with the mess that is left in the middle, neither obviously above the axis nor obviously below, but a bit of both and not much of anything. In a sense that middle group is one in which the sites stay fairly close to the mean, they are very well-behaved, and their variation is small. That in itself is a category, but it can be divided up by looking at the different shaped profiles.

The chapters of this book could be written in words only because the work on numbers had been done beforehand. I wanted to include a glance at the methods so that those who want to can follow them up and experiment for themselves. Without a mention of the methods any book is authoritarian and condescending; in giving only the results it implies 'I can tell you all about this, but don't overheat your brain by worrying about how it is all done'. In fact the 'how' is very simple indeed, as I hope this shows, provided you were not frightened off numbers at an early age.

Some people have called methods like these 'statistics': I disagree. The only things I have done are to add up, subtract, multiply and divide, and draw diagrams of the result. I admit to calculating an average, in fact a mean, but I really don't think this adds up to statistics – it is just the use of numbers.

Further reading

It is always difficult at this point to steer a useful course through temptations of different kinds. Any list of books and articles which would be helpful must suggest what can be understood and what can found in a reasonable library – and that removes a lot of possible recommendations.

Iron Age coins are best pursued in R. Hobbs's *British Iron Age Coins in the British Museum*, London (1996). Readable books on Roman coins include three classic works, all called *Roman Coins*. That by H. Mattingly (originally 1928) has been revised many times but it has a limited selection of pictures. There are more prints in the book by C.H.V. Sutherland (1974), and in 1978 J.P.C. Kent produced a version with luxurious pictures. My own attempt (1970) has an extended section on identification and a useful chapter on Alexandrian coins which I have not seen elsewhere, but the pictures are muddy and the text is fully stuffed with facts. *Roman Coins and their Values* by D. Sear (revised edition 2000) is a book to be used rather than read because it packs a large amount of information, and descriptions of many coins, into a small space.

If it is detail that you want then the only alternative is the ten volumes of *Roman Imperial Coinage*, H. Mattingly, E.A. Sydenham, R.A.G. Carson, C.H.V. Sutherland, and A.M. Burnett, Volumes I to X, (31 BC-AD 491) (1923-94). For the most commonly found coins in Britain, the copper coins of the third and fourth century, you could start identification with R. Reece and S. James, *Identifying Roman Coins*, second edition (2000). This will encourage you to move on to the best book of all, *Late Roman Bronze Coinage* by R.A.G. Carson, P.V. Hill and J.P.C. Kent (1960), but it is tough going if you start using it without help.

For coin reports from Britain you can compare five which are all rather different, and then dip in to any excavation reports that you come across. For the type of find and the detail of the thought and reporting, David Walker's report on the coins from the Sacred Spring at Bath stands in a class by itself: B. Cunliffe, editor, *The Temple of Sulis Minerva at Bath* vol. 2, pp.281-358 (1988). Then in order of publication: N. Crummy, editor, *Colchester Archaeological Reports 4: The Coins* (1987); A. Woodward and P. Leach, *The Uley Shrines*, English Heritage Report 17, pp.80-8 (1993); P.J. Casey and J.L. Davies, *Excavations at Segontium*, CBA Report 90, pp.122-64 (1993); and N. Holbrook, editor, *Cirencester Excavations 5*, pp.247-93 (1998). These still have to reach the archaeological standard and compactness of two reports from Carthage: the first is H. Hurst and S. Roskams, *Excavations at Carthage: The British Mission* Vol. I, 1, 171-81 (Sheffield 1984) and the second is H. Hurst, *Excavations at Carthage: The British Mission* Vol II, 1, (Oxford 1994). L. Allason-Jones and B. McKay, *Coventina's Well* (1985) is self explanatory.

The Colchester Report is the simplest way to find details of the work of Robert Kenyon on Claudian copies, John Davies on Barbarous Radiates, and Mike Hammerson on Constantinian copies.

On selected topics there is J. Casey's Shire Book, *Roman Coinage in Britain* (originally 1980), R.Abdy's Shire Book on *Coin Hoards in Roman Britain* (2002), and A. Burnett's British Museum Booklet on *Coins of Roman Britain*. There are several useful chapters in *Coins and the Archaeologist*, edited by J. Casey and myself (reprinted 1984). More wide-ranging is J. Casey's *Understanding Ancient Coins* (1986); and more numerical is N.S. Ryan, *Fourth century coin finds from Roman Britain, a computer analysis*, British Archaeological reports 183 (1988). A. Hobley's work is *An examination of Roman bronze coin distribution in the western empire*, no. 688 of the International Series of British Archaeological Reports (1998). My book on *Roman Coins from 140 sites in Britain* is mainly a list of numbers of coins from different sites and what you can do with them. It is available, like many other useful works, from Oxbow Books, Park End Place, Oxford. I set out the details for the method outlined in the appendix and applied it these coins from 140 sites in the journal *Britannia*, vol. 26, 179-206 (1995). Oxbow can also supply my book entitled *My Roman Britain* if you want to know what I think about Roman Britain apart from the coins.

The basic book on hoards is now A.S. Robertson, *An inventory of Romano-British coin hoards* (London 2000). The review by P. Guest and myself should appear in the *British Numismatic Journal* for 2002. The coins from the great hoard from Hoxne, as studied by P. Guest, will be published by the British Museum.

The pamphlet 'On the Things of War' is best found in M. Hassall and R. Ireland, editors, *De Rebus Bellicis*, no. 63 of the International series of British Archaeological Reports (1979). The *Satyricon* by Petronius needs to be looked at in the Loeb Classical Library edition where the Latin and the English translation are on facing pages. For the Gospels you have to have a Greek or Latin text because all translations play havoc with what was actually written. You do not need to read Greek or Latin, but you do need to see what coin word was originally used.

To find out about the coinage of the Roman Republic and the coinages of the Eastern provinces you can consult M. Crawford, *Roman Republican Coinage* (Cambridge 1974), and A. Burnett and M. Amandry, *Roman Provincial Coinage*, which is being written and published period by period and year by year.

For discussions of what is going on Empire-wide it is well worth looking through *Coin finds and coin use in the Roman world*, edited by C.E. King and D.G. Wigg (Studien zu Fundmünzen der Antike 10 Berlin 1996). It sounds forbidding, but there are many contributions in English, and there are lots of references that can be followed up. My article on Bronze coinage in Roman Britain and the western provinces in *Scripta Nummaria Romana, Essays presented to Humphrey Sutherland* edited by R.A.G. Carson and C.M. Kraay, 124-42 (London 1978) gives some thoughts not available elsewhere, and if you want to know what is going on in Rome you will have to consult 'A collection of coins from the centre of Rome' in the *Papers of the British School at Rome* vol. 50, p.116-45 (1982). I summarised information on groups of coins from different countries in R. Reece, 'Roman coinage in the western Roman empire', in the journal *Britannia*, vol. 4, p.227-51 (1973).

After this you will have to look through the review sections of four major journals which come out each year because they review all the important publications: *Numismatic Chronicle, Journal of Roman Archaeology, Britannia, Journal of Roman Studies.*

Index

Numbers in **bold** refer to figures

abandonment, 98. 103
abroad, chapter 6
accounting unit, 34
accuracy, 78
activity, 99
Adventus, 17, **5**, **20**
Aemilian, 24,
Africa, 134
ages, 30
Alexandria, 25, 26, **39**
Allectus, 23, 54, 56, 92, 99, 125, 142, **29**
Anglo-Saxon, see Saxon
anniversaries, 30, **36**, **40**, **colour plates 36**, **39**
Anonymus, 107
Antioch, 19, 23ff, 134
Antoninus Pius, 17ff, 121, **17**, **18**, **33**, **colour plate 1**
Aphrodisias, 134
Aquileia, 26, 36, 132, 137
Arcadius, **colour plate 43**
archaeological deposits, 135, 142
archaeological method, 100, 141
Arles, 26, 30, 32, 36, 57, 60ff, 87, 131, 137ff, **12**, **colour plate 41**
army, 17, 42, 116, 131, 134
Arras, 91
arrival, see Adventus
As 13, 18ff, 45, 81, 93ff, 112, 115, 118, 121ff, 135ff, **41**, **colour plate 1**
Asia Minor, 24, 25, 132
Athens, 134
Augustus, 14, 20, 38ff, 134, **1**, **43**, **colour plate 11**
Aurelian, 22, 47ff, 76, 141, **8**
Aureus, 15, 20, 117, **41**, **colour plate 22**
Austria, 133, 137

background, 100
Bagendon, 38,
bags of coin, 138
Balkans, 23, 24, 36, 61, 137
barbarian invasions, 69
Barbaricum, 78, 116
barbarous, 48
Barbarous Radiates, 48ff, 56ff, 65, 76, 84, 87, 91, 95, 115, 136ff, 141, **colour plate 20**
barter, 98
Bath, 115, 121, 123
Beaurains, 91, 109
Beirut, 136
Belgium, 137
Belo, 134
blank, 40, 122
Boudicca, 69
Britain, chapter 2, 44, 69, 80ff, 95, 114, 135ff, 141, **colour plates 2**, **40**, **41**, **42**, **44**
Britannia, 17, 121, 124, **5**, **17**, **18**, **colour plate 8**
British coinage, 38ff, 78, 120
British mean, 147
British pattern, 100

buildings, 17
bullion, 16, 33, 35, 65, 109, 111, 118
burial, 80, 92, 120

Caerleon, 104
Caerwent, 103
Caesaraea in Cappdocia, 25
Canterbury, 64
Caracalla, 19, **colour plate 15**
Carausius et Fratres Sui, 52, 130, **24**
Carausius, 23, 26, 51, 54, 56, 99, 125, 129, 141ff, **19ff**
Carthage, 103, 134
casting, 19, 40, 45, 85
casual loss, 84
central Empire, 48
centre, 109
change of standard, 15
Chester, 104
Chi-ro, 32, **16**
circulation, 64, 78, 122, 136, 138
Cirencester, 38ff, 102ff, 132, 145, 147
city coinage, 26
Claudian copies, 39, 42, 45, 99, **colour plate 3**
Claudius I, 15, 37, 40ff, 41, **colour plate 1**
Claudius II, 48, **colour plates 20, 21**
clipping, 63ff, 87, **30**
Clunia, 134
coin edict, 26
coin loss, 47, 57ff, 60, 63, 89, 99, 118ff
coin use, chapter 5, 57, 60, 63ff, 83, 88, 92, 97ff, 131
Colchester, 42, 82, 129
collectors, 91
Cologne, 21, 23, 48, 86, 136
Colonia, 24
comitatensian mint, 33
comitatus, 33
Commodus, 18ff, **34**, **43**, **colour plate 8**
Conimbriga, 132, 134
conquest, 37, 99, 104
Constans, 29ff
constant money loss, 96
Constantine I, 27ff, 132, **44**, **46**, **colour plate 29**
Constantine II, 29
Constantinian copies, 57, **colour plates 31**, **32-5**
Constantinople, 26, 28, 79, 134
Constantinopolis, 28
Constantius Chlorus 54
Constantius II, 29ff, **11**, **30, colour plate 30**
consulship, 17
continental mints, 48
continual offerings, 72
continuity, 99
copies, 39, 45, 48, 57ff, 62, 85, 87, 93, 109, 120, 138, **colour plate 31**, **32-5**
Corinth, 134
Cornwall, 105
Cotswolds, 62, 104
cottage, 102
Coventina's Well, 71ff, 121, 123
Crispus, 132
curation, 45
currency area, 92
Cyprus, 24
Cyrene, 25, 134, **colour plate 7**
Cyzicus, 26

Dacia, 24
Danube, 60, 86, 137
dating, 98, 143, **4**, **10**
De Rebus Bellicis, 107
debris, 103
demonetised, 95
Denarius, 13, 20, 25ff, 34, 42, 45, 51, 56, 72, 80ff, 84, 90, 94, 99, 110ff, 135ff, **2**, **3**, **4**, **41**, **colour plate 1**, **9**
Denmark, 78ff
denominations, 34, 38, 48, 94ff
deposition, 74, 95, 142
diagrams, 145

die-links, 61, 121ff, **colour plates 11-12**
dies, 40, 61, 85, 87, 121, 123, **7**
Diocletian, 47, 51, 54, 70, 76, 99, 111, 114, 126, 129, 141, **25**, **39**, **colour plate 26**
discarding, 47, 49, 62, 89, 91ff
distributing, 121, 125, 138
Domitian, 16, **4**, **43**
Double denarius, 20, 26, 76, **colour plate 15**
Drachma, **colour plate 7**
drift, 137
Dupondius, 14, 19, 113, 124, 125, 135ff, **41**

East Anglia, 103
eastern mints, 79
economy, 80, 92, 103, 128
Egypt, 25
Elagabalus, 19
engraving, 40, 57
error, 78, 123
Etruria, 24, 30
excavated deposits, 56, 89, 93, 95, 141
excavation reports, 82, 98, 142
exchange, 114ff, 128
exergue, 23
Exeter, 103
expected values, 95

Falkirk, 73
fallen horseman, 58, 65, **colour plate 36**
farmstead, 102
farthings, 91, 117
Fel Temp Reparatio, 31, 58, **40**, **colour plate 36**
field-walking, 93, 95, 141
fifth century, 58, 63ff, 66
Fishbourne, 101
Follis, 57, 130, **colour plates 1**, **26**
foreign prices, 117

forgeries (forging), 45, 85ff
fort, 89, 104, 145
Franks, 36
frontiers, 23

Gallic Empire, 21, 23, 48, 136
Gallienus, 20, 46, 48, **colour plates 17**, **18**, **21**
Gaul, 31, 39, 62, 69, 78, 80, 124, 138
Germany, 41, 48, 69, 78, 81, 124, 133, 137ff
gilded leather, 108
Gloucester, 103, 129
gold, 20, 24, 26ff, 30ff, 65ff, 128ff
Gospels, 109ff
Goths, 79, 138
Gotland, 79
graphs, appendix 2
Gratian, 32, **12**
Great Reform, 23, 26, 47, 54, 70, 95, 126
Greece, 134
Greek Imperial, 23
Greek, 24, 26

Hadrian's Wall, 104
Hadrian, 17, 42, 124, 5, 6, 43, **colour plate 14**
hand-outs, 34, 91, 109
heirloom, 45
Heraclea, 26, **colour plate 36**
history of coinage, 108
Histria, 134
hoarding, chapter 3, 42, 49, 56, 58, 60, 118
hoards, chapter 3, 44, 93, 95, 120, 132, **colour plates 23-4**
hoards, analyses of, chapter 3, 72
hoards, composition of, chapter 3, 72
hoards, interpretation of, chapter 3, 74ff
hoards, mixed, 83
hoards, unrecovered, chapter 3, 73ff, 77, 120
hostages, 38,

Hoxne, 87, 126
Hungary, 133

image, 27, 63
imperator, 14, 17, 40
imported goods, 117
incomers, 117, 131
inflation, 93, 109, 135
instant deposits, 72
intrinsic value, 20, 24, 26, 47, 49, 62, 65, 67, 81
Italy, 44, 48ff, 58, 95, 124, 134, 137

Jerusalem, 134
jewellery, 78
Julian, 30, **31**
Julius Caesar, 14, 38

largesse, 109
Latin, 24, 30
laureate, 26, **colour plate 28**
laurel wreath, 19
law codes, 95
legal tender, 94
legend, 13
libra, 27, 34
Libya, 25
Licinius, 28
local manufacture, 24, 121, 141
Loire, 136
Lombards, 36
London, 26, 54, 57, 92, 129, 132, 136, 137, **32**, **colour plate 26**
Low Countries, 48
low value coins, 83
Luxembourg, 132ff
Lycia, 25
Lydney, 58, **37**
Lyon, 15ff, 21, 26, 30, 36, 41, 57, 60ff, 86ff, 131ff, 137ff

Magnentius, 31
Magnus Maximus, 131, **32**, **colour plate 41**

Malta, 117
Marc Antony, 14, **colour plates 4-6**
Marcus Aurelius, 18, 122, **colour plates 1, 13**
market, 22, 47ff, 60ff, 83, 86, 103, 114, 141
Mauretania, 17
Maximian, 51, **colour plates 1, 25**
Maximinus, 20
mean, appendix 2
medallion, 54
medieval coins, 90
Mediterranean, 34, 44, 58, 60, 83, 130, 134ff, **colour plate 41**
Merovingian, 138
middlemen, 131
Milan, 23, 87, **colour plate 43**
military pay, 19
military sites, 42, 102, 118
military standard, 29, **10**
mineral resources, 62
Minerva, 40
mint-mark, 26, 28ff, 54, 60ff, 129, **9**, **26**
mints, 15, 29ff, 34, 36, 56, 120, 122, 129
minutum, 112, 114ff
modern coins, 89ff
money supply, 49
money-changers, 80, 118, 127
moulds, 40
movement of coins, 125, 131, 138

Nero, 15, 19, 41, 93, 121, 136, **2**, **3**, **43**
Nerva, 17
Nicaea, 26
North of France, 44, 48, 51, 81, 134ff
nummus (pl nummi), 34, 57, 65, 80, 126, 130, **colour plates 1**, **26**
NW provinces, chapter 6

obryzium, 33, **32**
occupation, 97ff, **colour plate 44**

Octavian, 14
offerings, 71ff, 112
official coins, 40
officina, see workshop
Ostrogoths, 36
over-striking, 42

Padua, 134
Palestine, 112, 114, 115
papyrus, 25
Patching, 64
pattern, 137ff
Pavia, 130, **colour plate 26**
peaks of hoarding, 75
peaks of non-recovery, 75
pension fund, 92, 112
Petronius, 113ff
Philip, 30
phoenix, 31, 58, **40**
plated coins, 109, **colour plates 8**, **10**
platinum, 33
pontifex maximus, **34**
Portchester, 101
portraiture, 24, 27, **14**, **19**, **21**, **colour plate 13**
post-Roman, 59, 63, 90
Postumus, 21, 42, 48, 83, **6**, **7**, **43**, **colour plates 16**, **19**
pottery, 41, 97, 143
pound, 27, 43
price edict, 27, 56, 111, 114
prices high, 116
prices, 114, 117
provinces, 26, 109, 113, 129
provincial symbols, 17
purchasing power, 20, 24, 26ff, 57, 99, 111
pusulatum, 32

Quadrans, 14, 18, 112, 115, 136, **41**

Radiate, 19ff, 26, 45ff, 57, 60, 76ff, 84, 86, 93, 95, 101ff, 125, 136, 141, **37**, **colour plates 15ff**, **28**
radiate crown, 19, **6**, **7ff**, **colour plates 15ff**
recycling, 19, 45, 64
refined gold, 33, **32**
refined silver, 32, 13
reform, 22, 58, 95
reformed radiates, 48, 76, **8**, **colour plate 1**
regional average, 143
regnal year, 17
reliability, 78
religion, 92, **46**, **colour plate 29**
residuality, 44
Rhine, 86, 135
Richborough, 62, 99
Roman Provincial, 23
Roman republic, 13, 17, 134, **colour plate 9**
Romania, 134
Rome, 13, 16, 23ff, 36, 41, 48, 86ff, 93, 103, 113, 121, 129, 132, 134ff
rubbish, 103, 141
rural sites, 102ff

sacra (sacred), 63, 118, 130
saecula, 30
safe-keeping, 93
Samuel Pepys, 81
Sardis, 132, 134, 136
Satyricon, 109, 113ff
Saxon shore, 99, 101, 105
Saxon, 63, 64, 66, 138
selection, 88
semi-official coins, 40
Semis, 14, 18, 136, **41**
Septimius Severus, 19
Sestertius, 14, 20, 45, 48, 65, 81, 83, 85, 94, 115, 119, 123ff, 128, 136, **5**, **6**, **17**, **33**, **34**, **41**, **43**, **colour plate 1**
Severus Alexander, 20, **43**, **colour plate 10**
Silchester, 38ff
silver content, 19, 27, 95

silver penny, 36, 90
silver plate, 44, 62
silver-copper, 27, 30ff, 46, 49, 51, 54, 59, 76, 125, 129, **4**, **colour plate 1**
single gold coin, 80
Siscia, 26, 60, 132, **colour plate 40**
site-finds, chapter 4, 49, 68, 76, 86, 93, 124, 143
Slovenia, 133
small change, 39, 83, 91, 93, 103, 114, 131, 141
soldiers, 23, 28, 49, 61, 126, 136ff, **10**
Solidus, 34ff, 126, **11**, **32**, **colour plate 43**
South Italy, 24
South of France, 44, 81, 134ff, 137
Spain, 15, 21, 36, 39, 41, 81, 134
stable currency, 92, 94
state servants, 49, 91, 136
stipendium, 114
stratigraphy, 142
striking, 85, 119, 121ff, 141
supply, 56, 62, 64ff, 83, 88ff, 93, 96, 99, 124, 136, 138
survey, 141
Sussex, 64
Sutton Hoo, 138

taxation, 34, 39, 46, 80, 115, 118ff, 126
temple, 89, 104, 145
Tetradrachm, 25, **39**
Tetricus, 21, 48, 136, **colour plates 19, 20**
Tetrarchy, 27
Thessalonica, 26
third-century gold, 78
Tiberius, 15, **42**
Ticinum, 130, 132, **colour plate 26**
token (value, rate), 13, 65, 66, 81
town, 102, 145
trade, 131
Trajan, 17, 42, **colour plates 1**, **7**
travellers cheque, 117
travellers, 137
treasury, **32**
Tremis (pl tremisses), 34, 36
Trevelgue, 105
tribunician power, 17
Trier, 21, 23, 26, 30, 32, 36, 48, 57, 60, 87, 92, 131ff, 137, **colour plate 42**
Trimalchio,113,
Troy, 134
Turkey, 134
type, 13, 28ff
typical coin finds, 101

Urbs Roma, 28, **9**
Usk, 82
Valens, 31, **14**
Valentinian, 31, 59, 61
Valerian, 20, 46
Verulamium, 102ff, 132, 142, 145, 147
Vespasian, 16, 42, 44, 121
Vetriano, 31
Victorinus, 21, 48, **colour plate 19**
Victory, **15**, **16**, **colour plates 38**, **40**
villa, 102, 104ff, 145
village, 102, 105, 145
Virgil, 52, **23**
Visigoths, 36
vota (vows), 30

wages, 56, 109, 110, 114, 117
weights, 65, 87, 95, 120
Winchester, 64
workshops, 29, **9**

year of the four emperors, 16
York, 105

Zilil, 132, 134